THE
Essential
Guide FOR
AREA LEADERS
in Retail

REVITALISING · RETAIL

THE Essential Guide FOR AREA LEADERS in Retail

by Alison Crabb

alison crabb

inspiring the humanity of business

Published by Alison Crabb Consulting
PO Box 202
Moonee Ponds VIC 3039

Edited by Scharlaine Cairns, Charlie C. Editorial Pty Ltd
Cover and internal design: DiZign Pty Ltd
Illustrations: DiZign Pty Ltd
Typeset in Avenir Next and Noto Serif
Printed in Australia

ISBN: 978-0-6489090-0-2 (e-Book)
ISBN: 978-0-6489090-1-9 (Paperback)

A catalogue record for this book is available from the National Library of Australia

Disclaimers:
Some of the names and identifying details in this book have been changed to protect the privacy of individuals.

The URLs appearing in this book were current at the time of publication. The author and publisher are unable to guarantee the ongoing currency of any URLs included in this book.

Foreword

In my very first week, as a brand new area leader for the Flight Centre Travel Group, I was sent to learn everything I needed to know from the 'best in the business'. She was rumoured to have the most amazing culture, the happiest people working for her – and outstanding results! Her name was Alison Crabb and I was lucky enough to spend a day on the road learning from her in that very first week in my new area leader role. That was the beginning of my many years of learning, development and self-growth, thanks to her.

Alison, or 'Ali' as she is known to me and to many others, is certainly a unique human being. She has many times described herself as 'an alien on this planet' and, in the most sincere way, I have to agree with her. There are few people in this world who can find the perfect balance between achieving business results, maintaining connections and living true to their own beliefs.

I was in Ali's leadership team from the beginning of her time as a state leader and saw her grow from strength to strength in that role, as my leader. Never afraid of a challenge, she embraced her role with a unique and refreshing style. For Ali, leadership is a way of life and people are the cornerstone of everything she does. She is disciplined, effective and passionate about everything and this shows in her ongoing success. Even when recognised as the best, with exceptional results and wide ranging respect, she has always remained modest and understated. People follow Ali because of who she is and what she represents.

This book is a taste of what has made Alison Crabb special to so many people. It provides the ideas and tools that area leaders need to simplify their roles and focus on what is truly important. The stories she tells are about real people overcoming real challenges and her concepts are built upon years of extensive on-the-ground experience. The suggestions and templates contained within these pages are the tried and practised methods employed by many successful area leaders whom she has led and these methods have been refined and improved over many years. They are combined here in an essential guide for all area leaders in retail.

Read these pages with an open mind and a desire to improve. Don't let your fear of change prevent you from implementing ideas that have been proven to work. Take notes, think, write plans and, most importantly, act. The strategies in this book will not only deliver better results for your business they will also make you a better and more respected leader.

Since that one day on the road, learning from her many years ago, I have been privileged to enjoy a powerful leadership journey and lifelong friendship with Ali, for which I am forever thankful.

Anthony Cowles
Former Area Leader Tasmania
Flight Centre Travel Group

Contents

Preface

I had almost finished writing this book in December 2019, just before the onset of the worldwide COVID-19 pandemic which represents possibly the single biggest disaster many of us will experience in our lifetimes.

The pandemic has had an unprecedented impact on all of us – socially, mentally and economically. Personally, within the space of one week, I went from having my business calendar completely booked with leadership workshops and coaching sessions to almost all of those bookings being postponed or cancelled.

The only positive I could find was that this allowed me the time and space to focus on finishing this book. There were times when I questioned the timing of releasing it – not because I had stopped believing in the content, but because I couldn't predict if what I knew from experience and the proven practical solutions I believed I could offer would even be heard by their intended audience in light of the overwhelming circumstances with which retailers would be dealing.

Naturally, due to the impact of COVID-19, the priority for every retailer is to make business and management decisions that will enable them and their businesses to navigate a way through these unprecedented times.

In supporting many of my retail clients during this crisis, helping them to determine how best to lead their businesses and take care of their staff, I realised that the strategies in this book are needed now more than ever. In fact, it became a matter of urgency for me to finish writing the book and get it into the marketplace of retail businesses and their leaders as quickly as possible. Now, more than ever, there is a need for businesses to reconnect, refocus and re-establish goals. Assisting with this became my purpose and helped me to stay motivated and focused amid the business chaos I was experiencing myself.

It is now my mission for this book that the strategies it contains will positively impact retail businesses and their leaders, helping to provide some positive direction now and during the economic recovery to come.

Acknowledgements

This book was written in a short timeframe, but I feel like the process of writing it has brought together all my work of the last 30 years. Without the support of many people this would never have been possible.

I would first like to thank my mum who dedicated her life to me, often working two jobs to provide for me and ensuring she gave me the best opportunities in life. She knew that this book was a work in progress but passed away before she got to see it completed. My mum was always very proud of me and would have been even prouder to have read these pages.

Throughout my career, more times than I can remember, my husband Shane has held the fort at home while I have been working or travelling. I know he thought I was mad to leave the safety and security of my corporate career to embark on setting up my own leadership consultancy company and venture into the unknown, but he has supported me and has been my number-one cheer squad every step of the way.

My incredible boys, Aaron and Matty, have taught me more than they will ever know. Although their observation of my displays of frustration resulting from bad service or poor retailing have made me the brunt of their jokes over many years, they are my world and mean everything to me. I know there are times when I have embarrassed them, but I also hope I have taught them that success cannot happen without great leadership and commitment. They are two incredible humans that I am proud to call my sons and are both forging their own paths in life. I know they will both make a difference in the world in their own ways.

I joined Flight Centre at the most difficult time in my life. If it wasn't for Geoff Harris, I am not quite sure what direction my life would have taken. He was the first person to ever truly believe in me and saw leadership qualities in me that I didn't see in myself. He has been my greatest role model, in life and in my career, and has shown me what it takes to be a true authentic leader.

My business manager Natalie McGee has been by my side helping to grow my business since its inception and has the most amazing 'Can do' attitude. I thank her for keeping on top of everything, for looking after all of our fabulous clients and for always exploring ways to do things better. I need her to know that that none of it goes unnoticed or unappreciated.

Scharlaine Cairns, my book editor and dear friend, has held my hand throughout the process as I embarked on writing this, my first book. Her patience and advice have been incredible and this book couldn't have happened without her support.

I sincerely thank Anthony Cowles, my 'voice of reason' and one of the greatest area leaders I had the pleasure to lead, who read these pages before they went to print. His constructive feedback was invaluable.

Some of the greatest times in my life have been spent with the area leaders I have worked alongside and who I have led over the years. I thank them for giving me the opportunities to learn the lessons of leadership that have made these pages possible.

I am also grateful to the readers who take the time to read this book and to be open to new ways of leading. My wish for them is that this book opens a world of opportunities for taking control of the ways they lead and the differences they want to make in their businesses and their lives.

Alison Crabb

Introduction

In 1995, after three years as a store manager for travel retailer Flight Centre, I was fortunate enough to be appointed as the first Flight Centre 'area leader' in Victoria. I was beyond excited to have been offered the new role and even more excited to accept it.

The region for which I was appointed area leader consisted of thirteen stores in Melbourne. Being a newly created role, there were no pre-existing job descriptions or systems manuals to guide me on the way to doing the job effectively. It was a case of trial and error; working it out as I went along. I relied on simply sharing with my team of store managers my own knowledge and experience.

Back then, there wasn't the benefit of professional backing from a big support team so, being full of enthusiasm for my new role, I took on a lot of the operational responsibilities myself. It was a huge growth phase for the company, so a lot of my time was taken up finding new sites, negotiating leases and appointing suitable store managers and consultants. To find suitable candidates to take on travel consultant roles, I recall bringing home bags of resumes that had arrived with me through the post (it was 1995 after all)!

As my workload and responsibilities increased, I could see that I wasn't achieving the results I wanted and that I had achieved as a successful store manager. I was frustrated, stressed and working long hours, feeling completely overwhelmed.

I just couldn't see where I could be going wrong. It was as if I was on a treadmill, constantly on the move but not getting anywhere, working harder and harder to try and get on top of everything but making no inroads. Desperately wanting to provide as much support as I could to my store managers, I found myself taking on even more, and more.

I knew this could not continue and that I needed to make some changes, but I just couldn't see where I was going wrong. I had been a very successful store manager, so why couldn't I achieve the same results on a bigger scale?

I was three years into the role, when I became pregnant with my first son, Aaron. I was thrilled to be a first-time mum and excited to start a new chapter, leaving my area leader role behind. I took maternity leave and, soon after, I had my second son, Matthew.

After a two-year break from my role at Flight Centre, I started to get itchy feet and felt ready to go back to work. I returned to Flight Centre and, making use of my teaching degree, took on a part-time role training all of the new store managers upon their appointment. It was this time that was to shape the next phase of my career.

Spending time with small groups of new store managers, allowed me the opportunity to really understand the role of an area leader from a store manager's perspective. I listened to what the store managers felt to be the most challenging elements of their roles, and what they felt they most needed to be successful in those roles.

What I found to be consistent about all the new store managers with whom I dealt was their desire to do well and their reliance on a significant amount of support from their area leaders to achieve their goals. As I listened, I identified with them and could really relate to what they were saying. I could hear my own thoughts and words in theirs. I understood for the first time why I had loved the role of store manager so much when it had been my role and what it was that had driven me to attain the results I had.

New store managers consistently shared with me how much their own individual success relied on the relationship they each had with their respective area leaders. They needed to know that their area leader believed in them, was there to support them and was committed to their success.

I loved this time in my career and this training role provided me with the knowledge I needed to step back into an area leader role myself and to do it with an entirely different approach and perspective.

After twelve months of delivering store manager training, I was to become the area leader of Flight Centre's most underperforming Victorian region (which also happened to be the most underperforming region in Australia). The region consisted of eighteen stores, of which only one was profitable. The other seventeen stores were all losing money. Some of the stores didn't have a store manager and, of those that did, there were a number of store managers who were not performing in their roles.

With a young family to consider, I had returned to the area leader role knowing that, if I was to successfully juggle a career and a family, I needed to find a better way of managing it all and to focus on the things that would matter most to deliver the best results – at home and at work. I needed to turn things around in my work role as quickly as possible.

I knew I was facing an enormous challenge, but it would also be a wonderful opportunity to revisit a previous role and do it differently, changing the way I operated and applying newfound knowledge from my time training the new store managers. I realised I needed to change the way I performed the area leader role the second time around.

One of the first things I needed to learn was how to structure my time more efficiently – daily, weekly and monthly – and to make all the time I spent count, allowing me to lead with maximum influence in the best ways possible.

I needed to focus on what I had discovered during my time spent training the store managers, employing to best advantage not only what I had learnt but also what I believed would make the biggest difference to the success of the stores in my area.

I knew I would have to make many changes to almost every aspect of the region, but I was up for the challenge. There is no doubt that the first twelve months were difficult, but they were also very exciting.

I needed to develop some new store leaders quickly and to recruit new travel consultants and have them trained as quickly as possible. Existing store leaders not only needed to raise their standards and the expectations they had of themselves and their teams but they also needed to feel valued and appreciated for the important role they played. Most of all, people at every level of the business in my area needed to feel valued and appreciated. They needed to feel connected to and personally invested in their team and to the region of which their store was a part.

As a business, we all needed to focus on valuing our customers and providing them with the best experience possible.

There was an enormous opportunity for growth. I was able to add an additional five stores to the region very quickly.

After two years of hard work, building a dedicated leadership team and addressing almost every aspect of the business, my region's group of

23 stores became the most profitable region in Victoria and the second most profitable region globally.

Results indicated that the strategies I had implemented over my two years in the role were working. The results were consistent and they were strong. Over the next two years the region continued to perform very well, achieving year-on-year growth.

After four satisfying and rewarding years of leading my region, I was asked to take on the role of state leader for Victoria and Tasmania, leading 149 stores and a team of six area leaders. These area leaders had been my peers, but I was being asked to be their leader.

The decision to accept the offer was not an easy one because I had worked very hard and invested a lot of myself into building my region, which was by then recording some fantastic results. I had come to love the people in my region and the store managers were like a part of my extended family. But state leadership roles are not offered every day and, if I hadn't taken the role then, who knows if and when it would have been offered again. So I accepted the role, with the blessing of everyone I had worked with in my region.

At this time, the performance of the business across the whole state was not meeting expectations. I began visiting many stores and speaking to many store managers. Those conversations revealed many of the same challenges and feelings I had heard years before. But I was confident, if I implemented the same strategies and held the same philosophies I had as a successful area leader, I could replicate the same good results as a state leader. It was a big job, but I was up for the challenge.

During the eight years that followed, I opened a further 80 stores and the team of area leaders in my region grew from six to ten. Over those eight years, the business in my region increased, from a profit of $18 million to $49 million, making it the most profitable division within the Flight Centre Travel Group globally.

I am incredibly proud of the results that were achieved by my whole team and even prouder of those area leaders who eventually took on even bigger roles within the Flight Centre Travel Group.

The experience of leading a large team of area leaders highlighted to me the pivotal role those individuals played in the results of the business.

They had the greatest influence on how stores performed and provided essential inspiration and motivation for their store managers.

From my years of experience, I have no doubt that area leaders have the most challenging role in a retail business, but it can also be the most rewarding role if done well.

I became convinced that the philosophies I had developed and implemented during my time at Flight Centre could be successfully implemented in any organisation wanting to improve results, in any industry. So, in 2016, after twenty-five years at Flight Centre, I made the huge life decision to start my own leadership company.

Since 2016, I have been combining and refining all of my knowledge, first-hand experience and philosophies, to create a range of workshops and programs to teach and support other business leaders to improve their results. I have also had the pleasure of working with many area leaders from retail businesses. All of the challenges faced by them are similar to those that I once faced and was able to overcome.

This book is designed to be a practical 'How to' guide, aimed at assisting area leaders to have more impact, achieve better results and make a difference to the organisations employing them. It also provides an opportunity for retail business leaders to reflect on how they are developing the skills of their area leaders and maximising the opportunities to lead them in a different more productive way.

It is intended that anyone working in retail will gain valuable insights from the pages of this book.

I am passionate about the important role area leaders play in retail and truly believe that the key to success and improved results lies with retailers starting to value and invest in the role and in the employees who fill it.

Retail leaders and managers need to understand the enormous influence an area leader has. There is no better time for those business leaders and managers to rethink how they value, invest in and empower those in area leadership roles to ensure maximum return for their own investment in their businesses. For this to happen, there needs to be a shift in thinking and a genuine understanding of the unique nature of the area leader role, as well as an appreciation of the specific skills required and the importance of investing in the professional development of area leaders to help them navigate their role more effectively.

How to use this book

This book is intended to support area leaders in fulfilling their roles. As I mentioned earlier, It has been conceived as a 'how to' guide containing strategies that will help you to find better ways to work.

All of the strategies in this book have been proven to work for me and for the area leaders I led during my eight years as a state manager. They have also helped many other retailers with whom I have worked in a training and coaching capacity since 2016.

Each chapter of this book focuses on a key aspect of the area leader role and you are encouraged to make your own notes throughout the book. Each chapter has a page on which you can write your 'Light bulbs'; by this I mean any points that suddenly made something clear to you and to which you can particularly relate, or that you would like to discuss or reflect upon further.

Each chapter also has a page on which you can note 'Actions', meaning points I have made to which you not only can relate but that also suggest strategies you would like to enact and implement in your region and in the way you work.

I encourage you to make use of those two pages in each chapter, so that you can start to create your own toolkit of ideas and actions.

Chapter 1

The role of the area leader

For the purpose of this book, I will use the term 'area leader' to refer to an employee whose role it is to oversee several retail outlets within an organisation. Different retailers may use different names to refer to the same role: 'multi-site manager'; 'regional leader'; or 'cluster manager', to name a few.

The number of stores a person who is employed in this role will oversee varies from retailer to retailer, as does the level of responsibility expected of the role within the organisation. Regardless of their title and level of responsibility, the fundamental role of people in this position will be similar, no matter the type of retail or the organisation, and the strategies in this book will apply to anyone performing that role.

Case Study: Mary

I would like to introduce you to Mary.

Mary is an area leader at a large retail chain. She oversees twelve stores, is very passionate about her brand and wants her region to do well.

Mary often feels stretched as a result of dealing with so many stores and she wishes that her teams would just do what needs to be done to deliver their daily and weekly budget projections.

She spends a great amount of her time dealing with people issues, often spending time recruiting staff and looking for suitable people to fill store manager roles.

Mary also spends a lot of time working to motivate staff to achieve budgets, answering store managers' questions and dealing with day-to-day challenges. She feels constantly stressed.

Due to her responsibility for a large casual workforce, Mary spends many hours managing rosters and making sure stores have just enough staff, but not too many, so staffing doesn't become an unnecessary expense for the business. This can be challenging and time-consuming when managing a seven-day roster every week.

Some of Mary's stores do not have store managers. She constantly feels like she is pulling people from one store to another to cover shifts.

In stores that don't have store managers, Mary struggles to hold staff accountable for results because she feels they are doing the best they can without a manager. She feels compelled to spend more time in those stores to provide additional support and this takes her away from her other stores. As a result Mary spends a great deal of her time driving between stores every day.

Mary doesn't have a pool of potential leaders ready to take on leadership roles because her staff members do not see leadership roles as attractive, with very little perceived reward for effort.

Motivating staff is sometimes difficult, because the staff is largely a casual workforce and members of staff do not see their work as a priority in their lives. This is frustrating for Mary because she feels under pressure from head office to achieve her budget goals.

After spending all day in stores, Mary's job continues when she gets home, where she responds to emails, reviews individual store results and sets up interviews aimed at filling vacancies.

Mary often questions why she is doing what she is doing and why people need her to motivate them to do the jobs for which they are paid. She was a very good store manager herself and can't understand why others can't do the job as well as she did.

You may have been to the circus and watched clowns who have mastered the art of keeping plates spinning in the air on sticks, concentrating intensely and focusing on each of the plates, careful not to let one of them fall and break. This could describe what Mary is attempting to do!

For the first three years of my own time as an area leader, I was like Mary. I experienced all of the highs and lows of leading in retail and I was that clown, trying to keep all the plates spinning.

I am sure, if you are an area leader, you too can relate to the difficulties faced by the clown. Do you have days where you feel as though you are working very hard to keep all of those 'plates' spinning? Are you rushing from store to store, juggling competing priorities, trying to meet the needs of all of your stores, managing your costs, and all while working hard to achieve sales targets? You can probably even see the funny side of the way you are overstretching yourself if you are able to visualise an image of yourself spinning plates.

The truth is you are probably working longer hours than you should to get everything done and keep everything on track. Just as it would be impossible for the clown to keep the plates spinning for days and days, it is impossible for an area leader to keep on top of everything, unless she or he finds a better way to do the job and deliver results.

As support staff are reduced and training budgets squeezed, area leaders are required to shoulder more responsibility than ever before. They are being given more tasks and responsibilities to perform while still under pressure to achieve their expected budgets.

The most successful store managers are often promoted to area leader roles, yet the leadership style and skillset required for a successful area leader are different from those of a successful store manager.

A store manager works in the same location every day, managing a frontline team made up of people who also work in the same environment every day. A store manager is able to build relationships with staff quickly and, being very familiar with the circumstances and work environment, is able to make decisions on the spot and in the moment, to assert immediate control over the situations arising within the store.

By contrast, an area leader works across multiple locations, each representing a different environment. An area leader needs to lead from a position of influence, by motivating and coaching the next tier down in the hierarchy of leaders at each of the stores which she or he visits. This requires a stronger leadership style than is required by a store manager. One area leader described the change from store manager to area leader as being like stepping up from primary school to secondary school where you have to think more independently and make more decisions of your own.

Once we acknowledge the difference between the roles of store manager and area leader, we can appreciate the need for a shift in mindset when taking on the role of area leader, to broader thinking and a focus on developing new skills and new ways of working. Even the most successful store managers need to appreciate the need for a change, to leading through influence rather than through control, which will be the key to success if they are offered and accept area leader roles.

If you have been a successful store manager and were able to build a great team, lead a good business and deliver great sales results, you should have developed the confidence and credibility to be a successful area leader. But you do need to recognise that the role of an area leader requires a unique set of skills - skills that are not learnt from being a store manager and that need to be taught and developed.

When you come to appreciate the differences between the store manager and area leader roles and become open and adaptable to learning the necessary new skills, you will quickly build confidence in your new role and in your ability to achieve the results to which you aspire.

If you read the respective job descriptions of a store manager and an area leader, you will realise that both roles work towards achieving the same outcomes. Typically, both job descriptions will include the following requirements.

- Lead, motivate and coach a group of people.
- Maximise financial performance and deliver budgeted results.
- Ensure an outstanding customer experience.
- Oversee day-to-day operations.
- Ensure that operational and brand standards are met.

However, the way store managers and area leaders go about the delivery of these requirements is very different and, as I mentioned earlier, each relies on a different set of skills and a different leadership style.

Leadership styles necessary for store managers and area leaders

High control

Low control

High influence

Low influence

Store manager   Area leader

The table below illustrates the key differences between the approaches and functions performed by both types of retail leaders.

STORE MANAGERS:	AREA LEADERS:
control	influence
tell	ask
train	coach
do	follow up/support
plan for now	plan for the future

A store manager can control results on a daily basis. Store managers are able to be hands-on and usually work from day to day, and week to week, focusing on the here and now. They are able to direct staff to do what needs to be done and can give on-the-spot training and feedback to the sales staff. They recruit, train and manage their own staff daily.

Area leaders spend more time in stores than they do in any other part of the business, so they have more contact with the staff and customers than anyone else in a middle-management leadership role within the business. When a new business strategy needs to be communicated and implemented throughout the store network, it is often the responsibility of the area leader to ensure its seamless roll out.

Area leaders need a broader range of skills than store managers. They need to learn to influence behaviours, to think more strategically and to be able to forward plan.

Area leadership: The most influential role in retail

I believe area leaders are more influential than any other leaders in retail.

Even though online retail sales are growing, 85% of all retail sales are still made face-to-face, in bricks-and-mortar stores. So, strategically, it makes good business sense to invest in your retail stores and in people, who remain your greatest sales avenue. It is vital that investment in frontline leadership become a bigger strategic focus for retailers.

All retailers work hard to improve their results. Thousands of retailers invest large amounts in enabling their teams of area leaders to spend most of their working days visiting stores. When salaries, on-costs and travel costs are considered, this can total millions of dollars.

But, dissecting the training and development budgets of most retailers, it would appear that there is least investment in training and developing area leaders to do their roles and deliver results. There is an assumption that a successful store manager can slip straight into an area leader role, without there being any consideration of the need for investment in teaching the new skills she or he might need to develop.

There is often far more investment in the induction and training of the newest staff members joining the business than there is for a new area leader who has just been promoted to the role.

It is not surprising that, without investment in training and acknowledgement of the change and focus required for the new role, a newly-appointed area leader could lack clarity in regard to that role, resulting in a choice to stay well within her/his comfort zone and to retreat back into the store manager persona that had been successful previously. Stuck in that comfort zone, the new area leader becomes the pseudo store manager for the day at each of the stores she/he visits as area leader, because this feels comfortable and makes her/him feel useful.

Area leadership: The most rewarding role in retail (when done well)!

Throughout my twenty-five-year career in retail, my time spent as an area leader was, without doubt, the best and most rewarding of those twenty-five years - building and being part of a community, and creating a sense of belonging and connection among a group of passionate people who were all working together towards a single vision and shared goals.

It was always rewarding to watch a new person join my regional team, usually starting as a novice travel consultant, then working their way to become a store manager and then advancing further to become a successful area leader.

I can recount many stories about young, keen, enthusiastic people building amazing careers, like the story about Adrian on the next page. This was the part of being an area leader that I loved most. Nothing gave me greater job satisfaction than watching a store manager from my region promoted to an area leader position and then watching their success in that role lead them to further promotion and more recognition. Decisions that I made as an area leader, supporting and encouraging new employees and assisting their development, benefitted not only the employee but also the entire business long-term.

Case Study: **Adrian**

I interviewed Adrian who had applied for a novice travel consultant position.

He was young, not long out of high school, and had limited experience.

He didn't quite have all of the necessary skills, mainly due to his youth and lack of experience, but he was full of passion and enthusiasm.

I couldn't give him a job right then, but my advice to him was that, if he went and had some further work experience and then contacted me again in twelve months, I would re-interview him.

Twelve months later, to the day, I received a call from Adrian. He said, 'Hi Alison, my name is Adrian. You may not remember me, but you interviewed me twelve months ago today. You said that I needed to get more experience. Well, I took your advice and I have been working for Optus in one of their retail stores. I have worked my way up to be a store manager and I am ringing to see if I can be interviewed by you again.'

After a long conversation, I said to him, 'Adrian, there is no need for me to re-interview you. I remember you and you have shown me that you have the attitude and enthusiasm to do well. You have the job!'

Not only did Adrian have an outstanding first twelve months in the role I employed him to fill with Flight Centre, he became a very successful store manager who was able to turn around underperforming stores.

Some years later, when Flight Centre expanded into Asia, the business needed skilled people to help set up the retail arm of the business in Singapore. They were looking for someone who could open a store, train leaders quickly and, just as quickly, be ready to move on and open the next store. Adrian was appointed to the role and did a fabulous job often wearing two hats, as a store manager and an area leader. He remained in Singapore successfully for a few years before returning to Melbourne.

Light bulbs

Actions

Chapter 2

The four categories of area leaders

When you think about your role as an area leader, what do you believe your purpose to be?

I am not referring to your job description. I'm asking you what you believe to be the true purpose of your role? Why were area leaders put on this Earth?

I want you to think beyond the role's job description and to reflect on the following questions:

1. Why do retailers invest resources to have area leaders in their businesses?

2. What do you believe the true purpose of the role of an area leader to be?

3. If I was to ask the CEO of your organisation the same two questions about the role of an area leader, how would she or he answer them?

Area leaders are a single point of contact for most of what happens at store level and they, most certainly, have the greatest influence on how well sales teams meet the needs of customers.

Area leader roles are roles of influence rather than of control. Area leaders influence the behaviour of all the store managers and staff for whom they are responsible. An area leader cannot be in every store every day (although some may try – remember Mary and the spinning plates in Chapter 1)! Fundamentally, area leaders are at the heart of a retailer's communication and are the source of all information relayed to stores from upper management. They communicate all areas of the organisation's support functions to stores and are the avenue for stores to provide feedback back to the providers of those various support functions.

To your stores, as an area leader, you are the face of the organisation's brand and you represent to them all facets of the business. Your attitude, body language, mindset and choices matter. What you model in your own behaviour will be the behaviour that is adopted and displayed by the personnel in your stores.

Area leaders assume a lot of different roles within the retail landscape: leader; motivator; problem solver; recruiter; mentor; and merchandiser – sometimes juggling several of these roles simultaneously (or spinning those plates)!

Every area leader wants to do a great job for the organisation but all of them can easily lose sight of their respective roles and, with the best of intentions, take on the duties of the store managers of the stores they visit. Having worked with many area leaders, I have seen this happen for a variety of reasons.

1   Sometimes it is because they genuinely want to help and support the store managers with their roles.

2   They may have a mindset that they can best support the store manager by taking this approach.

3   Maybe they are not sure of their own role, or how it enables them to make a difference so, having come from store manager roles themselves, they revert to what they know and with which they are most comfortable.

Expectations and support

From dealing with the hundreds of area leaders I have led and with whom I have worked, I have come to realise that area leaders require a well-developed capacity for providing to their store personnel what are best described as 'expectations' and 'support'.

Expectations: Ensuring that everyone knows what is expected of them in their roles. Area leaders should have a clear insight into what they expect of stores and personnel, and this needs to be clearly communicated to store managers and understood by them. Area leaders should also know what store managers expect from them.

Support: Area leaders need to provide store managers with the tools and training for them to be able to deliver on what is expected of them. Store managers need to feel they have everything they require to do their jobs and to deliver on those expectations.

There is definitely a correlation between the results achieved and how well an area leader has been able to convey expectations and provide the support necessary for them to be met.

I have found the differences in behaviour between area leaders can best be described using the four categories illustrated in the diagram below. As you read through each of the four categories and the behaviours and results listed in each region of the diagram you will probably be able to identify which description bears the most resemblance to your approach and which quadrant of the diagram you are leading from yourself.

Types of Area Leaders

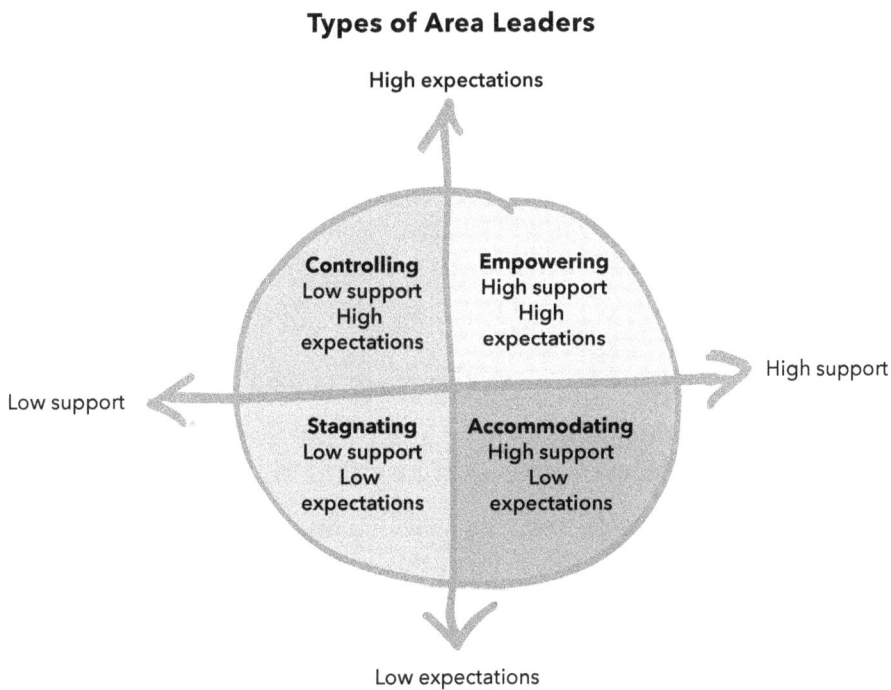

High expectations

Controlling
Low support
High
expectations

Empowering
High support
High
expectations

Low support

High support

Stagnating
Low support
Low
expectations

Accommodating
High support
Low
expectations

Low expectations

Defining area leaders by the support and expectations provided

1 THE 'ACCOMMODATING' AREA LEADER (HIGH SUPPORT AND LOW EXPECTATIONS)

Accommodating
High support
Low
expectations

An area leader categorised as 'accommodating' will be more focused on the environment of the stores in the region rather than on strategies.

Leaders from this category want to do a great job and want to ensure the personnel in their stores feel well supported. However, to achieve this, these area leaders often create additional work for themselves and, as a result, work longer hours to get the job done.

These area leaders often have a need to be liked and to please the people with whom they deal. As a result, they often find it difficult to hold store managers accountable for shortfalls in the achievement of budget expectations, fearing that doing so would damage their relationship with them.

They want to feel as though they are supporting their stores and, as a result, will often take on too much responsibility - taking on tasks and roles that should be performed by the store managers. They become the 'fixer' for everything and find it difficult to deflect responsibility back to the store managers where it belongs.

Store visits are focused more on relationships with the staff rather than on store results. These area leaders have a need for team harmony and they struggle to make difficult decisions for fear of being unpopular.

Many area leaders new to the role will display these types of attitudes and behaviours. If area leaders from this category stay like this for too long, it may cause frustration - not only for the area leader but also for the store managers.

Typical symptoms of 'accommodating' area leaders might be:

- difficulty holding their stores accountable for shortfalls in results and standards
- struggling to have honest conversations with store leaders and staff

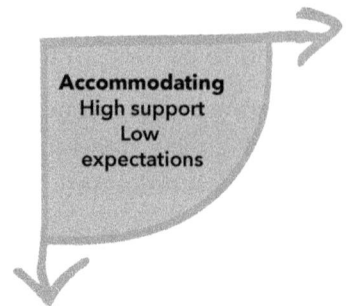

- inability to communicate clear expectations
- lack of adherence to brand standards by stores
- retention of underperforming staff and leaders.

The stores overseen by these area leaders are often nice places to work but they underperform in regard to budget projections and low standards are often accepted.

Store managers who are high achievers will often feel frustrated by how little their area leaders expect of them and the lack of higher targets for which to aim.

2 THE 'CONTROLLING' AREA LEADER (LOW SUPPORT AND HIGH EXPECTATIONS)

An area leader categorised as 'controlling' will be more focused on results rather than store environments.

Controlling
Low support
High
expectations

Leaders from this category will probably feel discouraged when stores in their region are not achieving their budget projections.

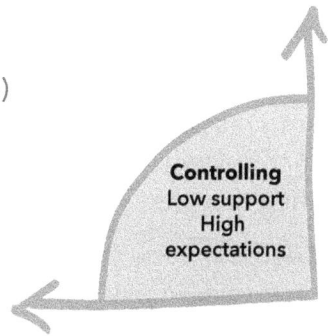

Often this type of area leader was once a very good store manager, leading to frustration when the store managers they oversee are not doing the job as well as they did. As a result, 'controlling' area leaders tend to put additional pressure on store managers, who then become fearful, demotivated and feel as if their voices are being disregarded and their opinions ignored. Store managers experiencing this feel that they don't have the support they need to achieve what is expected of them. This can create a 'them and us' mentality between store managers and their area leaders. When the pressure increases, it is likely that some store managers will want to step down from their positions or may leave the business altogether, leaving the area leader with the task of finding suitable replacements.

Typical symptoms of 'controlling' area leaders might be:

- focusing on key performance indicators (KPIs) and results but not providing store personnel with clear strategies for achieving them

- store managers being unclear as to what degree of autonomy they have and which decisions they are able to make independently

- accepting store managers doing only what is required of them without going above and beyond for the customer or the organisation

- an evident lack of teamwork and harmony in the stores in their regions

- a constant need to put out spot fires at store level that result from some of the symptoms listed above.

3 THE 'STAGNATING' AREA LEADER (LOW SUPPORT AND LOW EXPECTATIONS)

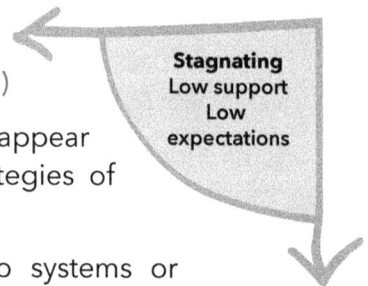

Stagnating
Low support
Low expectations

An area leader categorised as 'stagnating' will appear inconsistent across the environments and strategies of their region.

Leaders from this category probably have no systems or strategies in place.

They may have been in the role for some time and have already tried the different styles described in the other three quadrants of the diagram, but with no success.

These types of area leaders have lost sight of the purpose of their role and are unclear regarding the outcomes they want to achieve. It feels as if they are trying to keep all those plates we discussed in Chapter 1 spinning at once and will, at times, feel quite overwhelmed. They will be so overwhelmed that they find it difficult to stay focused on a task and will be constantly trying to 'tick boxes' as an indicator of achievement while feeling confused as to why they aren't actually achieving anything. They may develop a mindset that there is a lack of reward for effort in their role.

If they can't find ways to make their roles work for them, they will likely step down from their area leader positions or leave the organisation.

Typical symptoms of 'stagnating' area leaders might be:

- low staff engagement and little desire to achieve budgets
- high staff turnover, particularly of store managers

- disharmony or frustration among staff
- disengagement with the area leader role and its purpose.

4 THE 'EMPOWERING' AREA LEADER (HIGH SUPPORT AND HIGH EXPECTATIONS)

An area leader categorised as 'empowering' will be responsible for balance between the creation of a great working environment and implementation of strategies that achieve results.

Empowering
High support
High
expectations

Typically, those leading from this category deliver the best results. They are able to create and maintain high performing stores, regardless of their customer demographic or location. They take complete ownership of their region and its results.

These area leaders develop store managers who take full responsibility for results, deliver a consistent customer experience and create environments that make their stores great places to work. They demonstrate a genuine care for the organisation's brand.

Ultimately, these area leaders are able to achieve results by providing high levels of support in order to achieve the high expectations they have of their store managers and staff.

'Empowering' area leaders will:

- be highly driven to achieve
- deliver or exceed their budget expectations
- take ownership of and responsibility for their region and will believe in the company's goals and vision
- be passionate about the company brand and will find purpose in the area leader role
- be highly respected by their staff and their peers.

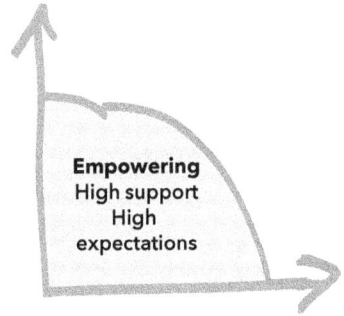

Moving between the categories of area leader

From my own research and experience of working with hundreds of area leaders, I have found there to be a correlation between motivational behaviours from leaders and great results in regions. However, 'empowering' area leaders don't suddenly appear. There is typically an evolution through the other categorical behaviours that occurs.

HOW 'ACCOMMODATING' AREA LEADERS CAN BECOME 'CONTROLLING' AREA LEADERS

Typically, area leaders start as 'accommodating' (high support and low expectations), wanting to support their stores and wanting to be liked – which results in wanting to please the people with which they deal, solving their problems and making everyone happy. Sometimes area leaders promoted from retail roles have become the leader of those who had been their peers and it takes some time to transition to this new role and the change in relationships it represents.

When results are not being achieved, the 'accommodating' area leader becomes frustrated. The role starts to feel difficult. The area leader, becoming uncertain of where to focus attention, starts to give even more to the role, working longer hours hoping that will achieve better results. As they work longer and longer hours to get the job done (trying to 'spin more plates'), resentment starts to build. As a result, these area leaders may move from the 'accommodating' category to the 'controlling' one.

HOW 'ACCOMMODATING' AREA LEADERS CAN BECOME 'EMPOWERING' AREA LEADERS

At the same point 'accommodating' area leaders find themselves dealing with the frustration that could lead them to become 'controlling' area leaders, they could also take the path of moving from the 'accommodating' category of area leaders to the 'empowering' category.

The decision to find ways to move from 'accommodating' to 'empowering' usually results from receiving helpful, honest feedback from a leader or mentor, which assists the area leaders to find a balance between the support given to their stores and the expectations they have for them. Recognising there is a need to change their mindsets and build their own self-esteem and confidence in their abilities often results from engaging a mentor or receiving supportive leadership from their workplace leader. This change of mindset could be all that is required for an 'accommodating' area leader to start to become an 'empowering' one.

HOW 'ACCOMMODATING' AREA LEADERS CAN BECOME 'STAGNATING' AREA LEADERS

It is at the point when a region is not achieving results that an area leader could lose confidence in his/her ability, becoming overwhelmed with the role and feeling that the rewards are not worth the effort being made. An area leader in this position could slip from being an 'accommodating' area leader to being a 'stagnating' one. This is a point at which the area leader could consider stepping down from the role or leaving the organisation altogether.

It is a real shame when this happens because the circumstances are avoidable. With specific training and mentoring, and a shift in mindset, a disillusioned area leader can make the transition to a more productive category of area leader and find ways to be successful.

The area leader category checklist

As you read through some of the behaviours displayed by the four categories of area leaders, I am sure you were able to identify with some of them. You may have even experienced moving through some of the categories throughout your own journey as an area leader.

On the following pages is a checklist aimed at helping you to identify which type of area leader category you are leading from. Once you have completed the checklist, the category with the most ticks will indicate the category that best describes your area leadership. This also will indicate the areas on which you need to focus in order to move into the 'empowering' category of area leader.

If you seek the support and specific training necessary for you to become an 'empowering' area leader, you will come to see the resolution of many of your area leader issues, as well as an increase in staff engagement and retention - and you will feel a genuine sense of reward for effort.

The more you can reach out to mentors and find ways to develop your leadership capabilities, the quicker you can grow and move towards being the best area leader you can be. Not only will you achieve better results, you will remain motivated to stay invested in your region and its people.

Area leader category checklist

Put a tick in the column provided beside each of the descriptions you think applies to you.

ACCOMMODATING	✓
I often avoid having honest conversations, even when I know they are needed.	
I feel the results I am achieving do not reflect the enormous effort I am making.	
I place more value on my relationships with my teams than on the results they achieve.	
I feel deflated when I can't solve a store manager's problem.	
Above all else, I have a need to be liked.	
I sometimes feel store managers take advantage of me.	
I accept poor performance too easily.	
CONTROLLING	
I become frustrated when store managers make excuses and don't achieve what I expect.	
I know my region's KPIs and ensure that my store managers know theirs.	
When visiting stores, I place a high emphasis on KPIs.	
I become frustrated when people only do the minimum expected of them and don't go above and beyond to deliver results.	
I value results over relationships.	
I am comfortable with replacing people if they are not achieving results.	
I become frustrated when store managers find it difficult to make decisions for themselves.	

STAGNATING	
I sometimes question whether this is the role for me.	
Often I cannot see how my role has a direct impact on achieving store results.	
I am unsure of the outcomes I want to achieve from my store visits.	
I sometimes feel I am 'ticking boxes' just to justify my role.	
I find it very challenging to create a plan and follow it through.	
I don't feel that my role rewards me for the effort I make.	
I feel disengaged in my role most of the time.	
EMPOWERING	
I place equal value on my relationships with store managers/staff and the results they achieve.	
My store visits are well planned with a clear purpose and outcome.	
I expect high standards in store presentation and brand standards.	
I feel that my store managers find me approachable.	
I have a good team of store managers who are experienced in their roles.	
I provide reward and recognition for the results my stores achieve.	
I work hard but feel rewarded and recognised for the results I achieve.	

This 'Area leader category checklist' is available for you to copy from my website: www.alisoncrabb.com.au

Light bulbs

Actions

Chapter 3

The performance pyramid

In 1993, I was very fortunate to travel to Egypt. Like most tourists, I was excited to visit the Pyramids of Giza. The Giza pyramids were built in 3000 BCE. Historical analysis tells us that they took 85 years to build. It is incredible that, thousands of years later, they are still standing in all their magnificence. But the reason they are still standing is that they were built on very strong foundations – a solid limestone rock plateau under the sand, with solid limestone and granite blocks used for the construction. The Egyptians knew the pyramid shape to be stable and strong and it is the strong foundations and the use of that strong stable shape for construction that has kept the pyramids standing to this day.

I will never forget seeing the pyramids for the first time and the profound effect it had on me.

I see the leading of great teams in business as being very similar to the building of a pyramid.

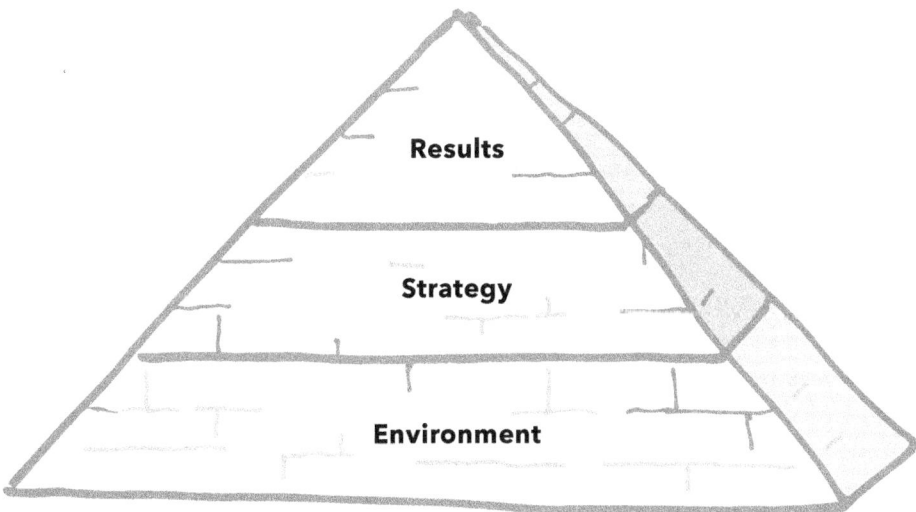

The foundation of a business needs to be built by focusing on the business environment first. It is the environment that provides the foundation for the strategy that will then be formulated. The strength of the business environment has a great impact on how well a business strategy can be designed and implemented. Results are achieved based on the success of the environment's foundation as well as on the strategy implemented.

Let's look at each of the layers of the performance 'pyramid' in more detail.

The environment

In business, or in any aspect of life, great teams must be built on stable strong foundations. In retail business, these foundations are part of what I call the business 'environment'.

The 'environment' of any team or business is often intangible – something that you can feel, but you can't touch or quantify. It might be hard to describe or explain but, if you pay attention when asking someone what they love about their job, the answer usually relates to the environment. It will most likely include a description of how they feel about the organisation and the leader for whom they work.

In his book *The Advantage: Why organizational health trumps everything else in business* (Jossey-Bass; Wiley, San Francisco, CA, 2012), Patrick Lencioni calls what I call the 'environment' the 'health' of the organisation. Lencioni says of organisational health (on page 3 of his book) that:

> *It's not at all touchy-feely, and it's far bigger and more important than mere culture. More than a side dish or a flavor enhancer for the real meat and potatoes of business, it is the very plate on which the meat and potatoes sit.*

I will never forget my very first one-on-one discussion with Flight Centre Travel Group's co-founder Geoff Harris when I first joined the company in 1990. I was only into my third week on the job and had never worked in travel before, so I was still learning all of the systems and products and getting to know my team. Geoff was visiting my store and, after spending time with my store manager, he asked if he and I could leave the store for a coffee. I was a little nervous and wondered why on Earth the 'big boss' wanted to speak with me. I was the newest member of the team and was just hoping that I hadn't done anything wrong.

Geoff proceeded to ask me a lot of questions, not so much about the job but about me – as a person. We discovered we both had a love of sport, in particular AFL football. He asked me about my goals and aspirations and where I wanted to take my career. To be honest, I had never really thought about it before but, if I'd had any doubts about my decision to join the company, they were alleviated within fifteen minutes of that conversation. From that moment on, I was all in.

Geoff would visit each store once a month and, after spending time with the store manager, would always spend time one-on-one with various team members.

In about my third month, Geoff and I had another coffee. This time he asked me for feedback. He said, 'Now that you have been around for a few months, I am interested to know, what you think we can do better as a business.'

I thought about it for a couple of minutes. During my days at university I had worked part-time for a fashion retailer. Each week the store window displays would be changed to feature new stock. At the beginning of each week, I would look forward to arriving at the store to see what was in the new window displays.

I shared this with Geoff, saying, 'As retailers of travel, I don't think we maximise the opportunities offered by our store windows.' He slowly began to nod in response and started writing notes about what I was saying.

Within weeks, store windows across all fourteen Victorian Flight Centre stores had new window banners that were rotated monthly.

I felt really gratified that an idea from a three-month employee had been taken on board and implemented. I felt valued, appreciated and listened to. I also knew that this experience would be something I would never forget and it became a core contributor to my own leadership philosophy.

I am convinced that building a great business must start with the business environment but, often, this aspect is the most neglected. If you want to attract great people to your organisation it is necessary to have an environment in which people want to work. How people feel about the environment of the business will determine how engaged they are when working in it and whether they will choose to stay or to leave your business.

Concentrating on sales and KPIs will never attract the best people or help you retain them. It is the way people feel about the organisation and about their leaders that will have enormous impact on the morale of the team – and it is the morale of the team that impacts on how well your team looks after its customers.

The role of every business leader should be to create a great environment of which everyone wants to be a part.

The strategy

As well as a great environment, a successful organisation needs a great strategy - a simple, easy to implement plan of action designed to assist with achieving the goals of that organisation.

A business strategy is like a road map. We need to know where we are and where we are aiming at going. The strategy is the road map outlining the way to get there. Having a clear, workable strategy creates focus and direction, as well as bestowing ownership and accountability on everyone tasked with implementing it.

Retailers invest heavily in their marketing, their product, their technology and their strategy for dealing with customers. All of these are vital for the sustainability and growth of the business.

Although the business will have an overarching strategy, each leader within the business should be able to take the organisation's business strategy and apply it to their own business plans. They can operationalise the organisation's strategy in their own approaches to the business and have some level of accountability for the strategy's implementation.

Results

Every organisation is focused on achieving results. Whether it is a sales target, a profit target or a growth target, there is always an outcome that everyone in an organisation is aiming to achieve.

Having observed many organisations in many different industries, I have noticed that there seems to be a huge emphasis and focus on discussing results. Most executive meetings and store staff meetings are consumed with focusing on KPIs and this takes up the majority of the discussion time. Hours of store visits and one-on-one discussions (commonly referred to as just 'one-on-ones') are spent trawling through KPI reports.

Results are an outcome and, if you think about it, you can't actually control your results with certainty. What you can control is where you choose to focus. My experience has shown me that the most impactful areas on which to focus are working on improving your environment or working on improving your key business strategies. The diagram below is a simple representation of the idea that focusing on the environment and strategies indirectly focuses on results.

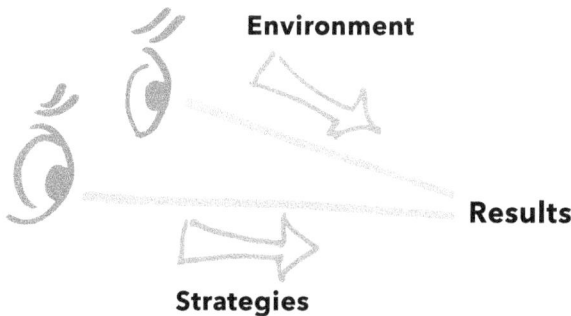

Environment

Results

Strategies

Favourable results are what we are all in business to achieve. However, as much as we want to achieve those results, they are really the outcome of how well we manage to provide a happy and productive workplace environment and how well we can implement the strategies that we have agreed with our staff will further the business.

I often say that you can't actually directly control your results, but what you can control are the things that impact on your workplace environment and strategies. Recognising that results are dependent on the environment you create and the strategies you implement will make you realise that more discussion time during in-store visits and one-on-ones should be focused on these areas.

Environment, strategy and results all working together

The ability to achieve results through implementing your strategy will rely heavily on the health of your environment. You could have the best strategy in the world but, if there isn't alignment and a common focus across the members of your leadership team, who feel collectively responsible for achieving common goals, you will spend a lot of your time trying to get everyone on board and working for the same ends. I doubt that dealing with these kinds of issues was part of your business strategy!

Your results are an outcome of how well you have managed to provide an environment of which everyone in your organisation wants to be a part. When your staff are working in a positive, cohesive environment, their engagement will be increased and your strategies will be easier to implement.

The region health checklist

To help you determine how well your region is performing in the areas of 'environment', 'strategy' and 'results', a checklist is provided on the following pages for you to complete.

When you think about your role as an area leader, what do you believe your purpose to be?

The descriptions in the checklist are designed to help you identify what you might need to focus on to improve your leadership and to achieve better results. Be as honest as you can be when completing it – this is not about being right or wrong! As well as a column for placing a tick beside the descriptions you think apply to you, there is also a column provided for you to make notes.

Sometimes in business, we know there are opportunities for improvement and to achieve better results. It is just a matter of knowing where to focus to make the most of the opportunities and achieve those results. There are plenty of strategies in this book to help you improve in all of the areas listed in the checklist.

Region health checklist

Put a tick in the column provided beside each of the descriptions you think applies to you. Add notes if needed.

ENVIRONMENT	✓	NOTES
I have a clear understanding of the type of environment that maximises my team's performance.		
I feel a strong sense of connection to my region and treat the business like my own.		
I ensure my store managers feel valued and appreciated for the work they do.		
I know about my store managers' lives away from their work.		
I know my store managers' hopes and dreams.		
I find ways to show my commitment to helping each of my store managers succeed in their role.		
A high level of mutual trust exists between me and each of my store managers.		
I ensure the part-time and casual staff in my region feel valued and appreciated for the work they do.		

(Continued on next page)

I spend time getting to know my part-time and casual staff and their hopes and dreams.		
I create opportunities for my store managers to work together to develop and benefit from connection and a sense of belonging.		
Regardless of their roles, I create opportunities for staff across the region to spend time together to create a sense of community.		
I create opportunities for my team to provide feedback and share ideas.		
STRATEGIES	**✓**	**NOTES**
Everyone in our team shares and owns the same clear vision for the business.		
A set of core values is used to help guide the making of decisions in the business.		
Our business has clear strategies in place to achieve goals that are known and owned by everyone in the team.		
All of my team members know exactly what is expected of them in their roles and they meet those expectations.		
A measure of our success are the KPIs that are in place, aligned to the organisation's goals and owned by the team.		
There are reliable communication systems in place to ensure everyone is informed about what is happening in the business.		

	✓	NOTES
There is a workable plan in place to continue to develop the leadership attributes of members of my team.		
I have a workable plan in place to identify and develop future leaders in the business.		
I spend time planning and preparing for my store visits so that they are purposeful.		
I have a plan in place that helps prioritise the way I schedule my store visits.		
I spend time working on my part in the business and on a plan to help keep me focused on my goals.		
There is reward and recognition to acknowledge great performance across my region.		
RESULTS	✓	**NOTES**
I know which KPIs are the key drivers of results in my region.		
I spend time at the end of each month to assess my results.		
I create a 90-day and 30-day plan that help me stay focused on my goals.		
Results of my region are communicated across my teams.		
The store managers in my region know their budgets and take ownership of their results.		

This 'Region health checklist' is available for you to copy from my website: www.alisoncrabb.com.au

Once you have completed the checklist, ask yourself whether completing it has changed the way you perceive your role and its purpose? You might find that you already have more clarity regarding what might be missing from the way you are fulfilling your role and where you could focus to achieve improvement.

From what you have read so far and from competing the checklist, you might already have some 'light bulbs' and 'actions' to note on the pages following.

When your environment and strategies are working together, results will take care of themselves.

In the following chapters, we will start to work through some of the key areas that will help you improve your business environment, implement some key strategies and improve your results.

Light bulbs

Actions

Chapter 4

Building the environment

In my second stint as an area leader with Flight Centre, I took over the most underperforming area in Australia. It was made up of eighteen stores of which only one was profitable. Seventeen stores were losing money – some a significant amount of money!

Before I visited any of the stores, I spent time looking at their KPIs in an attempt to understand what could be causing the results and, more importantly, what needed to be fixed to turn things around. What I saw was alarming!

Of Flight Centre's five Victorian regions, the region to which I had been appointed had the lowest sales per consultant. It also had the highest staff turnover of all Flight Centre's regions throughout Australia, which resulted in a lack of experience among the consultants, contributing to a high level of customer complaints and high costs.

I went from store to store to meet each of the store managers and consultants and had one-on-one conversations with everyone in the region.

The feedback from every individual was consistently the same. There was no shared vision and no goals for each team to work towards. There was a lack of teamwork and cohesion in the teams. I found the best way to describe it as, 'Everyone came to work, sold some travel and went home.'

The stores were messy and appeared disorganised, with not even the most basic systems in place. It became very clear that there were a lack of standards and lack of pride in the brand across the teams.

The high staff turnover meant there were many new consultants, resulting in a lack of the product knowledge critical for delivering the best customer experience. Considering the fact customers were coming to us for our travel expertise, this was far from ideal.

Consultants felt frustrated because they were not being given the support they felt they needed to learn their roles and to be successful at them. Many staff members felt they were constantly spending much of their time training new staff due to the high staff turnover, which was taking them away from their own work.

From speaking with many of the store managers, I discovered they felt lost and directionless. Some spoke of their lack of motivation to even become a store manager in the first place but they had felt pressured to take on the role because they were the most experienced in their stores.

What was evident was that, despite many new people joining the company with a genuine passion for travel and a genuine desire to have an outstanding career, their hopes and dreams were quickly dashed once they started in their roles.

I also saw that some individuals had low standards and couldn't be part of the culture I wanted to create.

With what I had uncovered, I began to construct a business plan to give myself the best chance of turning things around. I reflected on what I had learnt from my time training the new store managers.

What had resonated most with me was that the store managers wanted to feel heard, supported, valued and connected. They desperately wanted to have a sense of belonging to a community (or, as I describe it, a 'tribe'). They wanted to feel part of a team and this seemed to matter more to them than anything else.

I could see that, while addressing all of the organisation's strategic challenges was going to take a little longer, addressing the way people felt about their roles and the important work they did could be addressed really quickly. Creating an environment in which people felt valued, appreciated and part of a community was going to be the foundation I laid for rebuilding the region.

I have seen many organisations, with clear and well-documented strategies, but where implementing those strategies proved a struggle - often as a result of shortcomings in the business environment.

Since 2016, I have worked with many retailers, listening to the challenges they are facing and want to fix. Those challenges usually relate to a lack of growth and, in some cases, a drastic decline in results relating to areas such as profit, sales growth or market share. The cause or major contributing factor for these problems is usually perceived as lying with the business strategy of the business - rising costs, declining margins, increased competition, or online disruption.

All of those are usually correct if we look at the key measures of the business. However, as I start to work with retailers to uncover the root cause of these strategic issues, we find the causes nearly always relate back to the business environment. For example, some of the rising costs in the business might be attributable to high staff turnover creating the need to constantly recruit and train new staff. This would also impact on the level of experience and knowledge possessed by the staff and would impact their sales ability.

I have read many exit interviews in an attempt to understand why staff leave their organisations. Consistently, I have found that decisions to leave do not usually result from the strategic direction of the organisation but from the environment. I am yet to hear of anyone leaving their place of employment due to the organisation's marketing plan or product strategy.

Typically I read comments like:

- 'I didn't get along with my manager'
- 'I felt like a number'
- 'My shifts were often cut at short notice, which impacted my income'

- 'I didn't feel rewarded and recognised for my work'
- 'I was expected to achieve sales targets but didn't receive the training to do so.'

What most impacts people's level of happiness at work is the relationships they have in the workplace.

Commonly, underlying issues seem to relate to how staff members feel about their leaders and, ultimately, that affects how they feel about the environment of the organisation.

Leaders are always responsible for the environment of the business they lead. In a recent report by Deloitte (*Access economics: Soft skills for business success*, Sydney 2017), it was highlighted that, if leaders want to elevate the employee experience, there is an increasing need for them to learn the softer skills of leadership, such as empathy and an understanding of the importance of relationships and connection.

Environment versus culture

When I speak to leaders of retail businesses, I have found it can be easy for them to confuse 'environment' with 'culture'.

The environment is what often contains the intangible qualities of the business. It is about how people feel when they come to work. The leaders of the business create the environment, so the environment can only be as good as the leaders of the business.

The culture is the product and result of the environment. If a business has a cultural problem, it will have an environment problem – and if a business has an environment problem then, ultimately, it has a leadership problem.

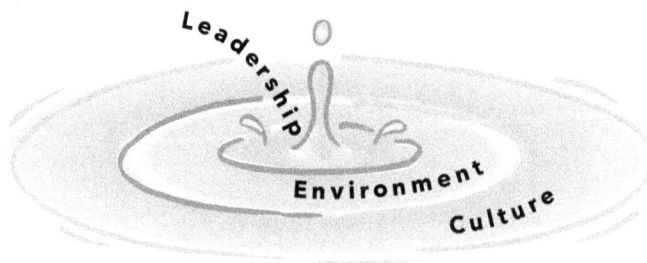

Leaders create the environment and the environment creates the culture. The more effort put into the environment of your business, the better its culture will be.

The best results are achieved when the business environment and strategies are working together. A lot of the strategies that I will share in this book impact on the environment.

Building an environment of which everyone wants to be a part

Some of the steps I took when aiming at building an environment that became the catalyst for turning around results are:

1. a common vision (achieving alignment through storytelling)
2. building and valuing relationships
3. harnessing connection
4. creating ownership
5. valuing and appreciating people (all of them).

I will elaborate further on each of these steps on the pages following and also in Chapter 5, 'Building strategies', so that you can see how the business environment and business strategies work together.

1   A common vision (achieving alignment through storytelling)

I felt I needed to create a shared vision for my region and for what the region stood. For the vision to be something which everyone in my region could relate to, focus on and believe in, it also needed a compelling story to support it.

This vision and its back story would be crucial for setting the standards and behaviours I expected and that would build our success.

The vision supported by almost every other business I had seen was focused on the business itself and where that business was heading, but I felt that I needed to create something that was about people - a vision that was about working together to build something special. Our vision had to be represented by more than just a bunch of statements that looked good on the wall. The following is the original unedited version of what became the shared vision of my region and the story behind it.

OUR VISION: 'IT TAKES A VILLAGE TO RAISE A CHILD'

IT TAKES A VILLAGE TO RAISE A CHILD

This ancient proverb teaches us eternal truth.

No man, or family is an island. We'd all like to think we live in a place where people care about others- where people pitch in to help when things get rough.

It's pretty awful when you feel like you are all alone and whole world is against you. Life is a lot easier when; you are part of a network of friends and family, a community, a village.

It does take a village, to raise a child and weather the storms of life. If we want that kind of support, the place to begin is with ourselves. Community, like charity, begins at home.

If you don't know someone in your area, you can take the initiative. You can go and chat to a new person and welcome them; you can ring someone that has had a tough month and offer some support. You can reach out to your own team and start building community. You can make a difference to someone else.

There are many things that we just don't have much control over. But building a great area is something that we can do, right now, in the place where you are now.

You start building a good neighborhood when you yourself decide that you will be a good neighbor.

The message of the African proverb that inspired this 'vision' means that an entire community of people must interact supportively with children for those children to grow and experience a safe and healthy environment.

This vision is about support for each other, not about a paternalistic dominant authoritarian leadership style. We are all adults, not even metaphoric children, but establishing a strong community support network helps us to all be better adults and meet our adult responsibilities.

This vision drove every decision we made in the region and created the standards we all came to expect of ourselves and of each other. Our vision was communicated, utilised and reinforced at every opportunity when we were together.

2   Building and valuing relationships

Initially, every one of my store visits was focused on building relationships. I felt this was imperative for turning around results.

In order for me to get everyone on board with new strategies, behaviours and standards, I first needed store managers and consultants to trust me. Trust would only be built if I invested time in building relationships with everyone, from the most experienced store manager to the newest consultant. I invested time in getting to know each person during one-on-one discussions. Initially, I did not ask each of them much about their work role but more about themselves: their motivations; and their hopes and dreams for their careers. I learnt about their families and their lives outside of work, as well as sharing with them a lot about my own life and my passions. I related this back to my own experience as a novice travel consultant and the impactful conversations Geoff Harris had with me. It was the care Geoff had showed for me and the leadership that he had modelled to me that taught me the importance of this kind of interaction as a valuable strategy.

3   Harnessing connection

Not only was it crucial for me to develop trusting relationships with store managers and consultants, it was crucial that store managers had trusting relationships with each other and with their teams.

I believe that area leaders can spend too much time dealing with people problems - whether the problems be conflict, performance or relationship issues within teams, all of these prevent the establishment of a connected environment and are a cause of teams not working together. I believe that most staff turnover is due to unhealthy relationships within the workplace environment. Whether the relationship issue is with a team member or the team leader, if there is a lack of connection and trust, people will leave.

A group of store managers who are cohesive and aligned to a shared vision and goals will have an enormously positive impact on the whole environment in your region.

I found ways to ensure that the store managers spent time together, not only working on their business but also building connections with each other, so they felt supported not only by me but also by their peers. Store manager meetings are a great way to connect and learn from each other (more on this in Chapter 10). The store managers were crucial to building the community I wanted to create.

At the start of every month I met with store managers and assistant store managers. These meetings became the vehicle not only for building connection but also for creating opportunities for team development. The meetings with assistant store managers provided an opportunity for me to see who was ready to step up and enabled me to begin building a community within the leaders of the future.

4   Creating ownership

If we want leaders to achieve results, they first need to take ownership of the results for which they are aiming. Each leader needs to have the mindset that she or he 'owns their business'. This need not be physical or financial ownership, but it does need to be 'spiritual' and psychological ownership.

To meet my regional budget goals, rather than giving each store manager a target for making her/his share of the total target figure, I would ask each store manager to develop her/his own store budget goal, ensuring they each had ownership of their own target. They each needed to make decisions for 'their' business; decisions that would be in line with their budget goal and attaining it. Not only did this create ownership, it also improved the business acumen of the store managers (more on this in

Chapters 8 and 11). I would then check that the total of all the stores' target figures had reached my overall regional budget goal. More often than not, the total exceeded the regional goal because each store manager wanted to achieve more than I had expected. Most importantly, each store manager had committed to a target and had striven to achieve it.

5   Valuing and appreciating people (all of them)

I truly believe that everyone comes to work to do a good job. Whether they are the store manager, or a part-time or casual staff member, everyone needs to be valued equally. This means leaders need to have one-on-one discussions with part-time staff, getting to know them just as well as they know full-time staff.

I have never considered the worth of anyone based on their role; be they store manager or part-time or casual staff member, everyone should be valued equally.

If you treat your staff as if they are just numbers, they will behave that way and this will impact on how customers are treated and, ultimately, on morale. Noticing the little things that someone does and acknowledging that will pay off. Remembering the name of someone's partner or the names of their children, or remembering an important date or event in their lives can make a real difference.

I hold the philosophy that your staff are humans first and employees second. It is about *who* they are, not *what* they do or the roles they fill.

I have always remembered the following adage and it has been a key influence on how I have made many business decisions:

> *Profit is the measure of how well you meet the needs of your customers. Your customers are the measure of how well you meet the needs of your people.*

Light bulbs

Actions

Chapter 5

Building strategies

In Chapter 4, I have already shared some of the ways of building a positive environment that were instrumental for me, as an area leader, being able to turn around my region. You could say that creating a great environment is actually a great strategy in itself – and you would be right. But building an environment and building strategies are slightly different.

'Environment' in a business is an intangible and is difficult to measure and quantify. 'Strategies' are easier to identify and easier to measure.

I have already emphasised the importance of building a great workplace environment. Having great strategies is also crucial but I need to stress that great strategies alone will not achieve great results.

I also need to highlight that maintaining a great environment, once established, is in itself an ongoing strategy. This is not something usually focused on when an area leader begins to lead a region, but it is something that should be focused on consistently and at every opportunity.

When you have a great environment, implementing strategies becomes easier because your teams are happy, engaged and want the organisation to do well. They feel invested in its success.

Patrick Lencioni (in the subtitle of his book *The Advantage*, already referred to in Chapter 3) says 'organizational health [which I refer to as the 'environment'] trumps everything else in business.' By this I interpret him as meaning that the achievement of the best results will happen when the business environment and strategies are working together.

As you read through the following chapters, it may surprise you to see that there isn't a chapter specifically dedicated to the customer experience or how to improve your customer service. That is not to say that I don't believe this to be important. I am a believer that the customer experience can only improve if the staff experience is focused on first. What matters to customers is how they are treated by staff. When morale is high and staff feel valued and appreciated for the work they do, that has the greatest impact on how well they look after customers. Area leaders are in a position to have the biggest impact on the staff experience, which also impacts on the customer experience.

In the following chapters, I will share some of the most effective key strategies, which have proven to work. Each chapter is dedicated to one of the following strategies.

- Strategy 1: Prioritise and manage your time (Chapter 6)
- Strategy 2: Maximise your store visits (Chapter 7)
- Strategy 3: Deliver on your store visits (Chapter 8)
- Strategy 4: Engage your part-time workforce (Chapter 9)
- Strategy 5: Have meetings that matter (Chapter 10)
- Strategy 6: Develop your business acumen (Chapter 11)
- Strategy 7: Develop your future leaders (Chapter 12)

As you read each of these chapters, it would be helpful for you to have the right mindset. Author Carol Dweck, is 'a pioneering researcher in the field of motivation, why people succeed (or don't) and how to foster success' (https://www.ted.com/speakers/carol_dweck). She is a respected expert when it comes to mindset and believes we either have a 'fixed mindset' or a 'growth mindset'.

A 'fixed mindset' refers to the belief that we only have a certain skillset and are only capable of what comes naturally. For example, if you are a good swimmer but not a good runner, then a fixed mindset would accept that is just how it is - it's how you were born and you can't really do much about it. This mindset means that there is no opportunity to change or to improve.

A 'growth mindset' refers to the state of mind in which our beliefs tell us that we can keep growing and developing if we are open to change and looking for possibilities. If we are open and prepared to try something different, then we have the capacity to improve and grow.

As you read through each of the following chapters it would be helpful to adopt a growth mindset and be open to thinking about how you could try implementing some of the strategies discussed. Not only would this mindset be helpful for you in your role, but it would also benefit your store managers to open their minds to the same possibilities.

If you are delivering great results already, then I would say that what you are doing is working fine and the following chapters might just represent an interesting read, or might provide the icing for an already 'well-baked cake'. But, no matter how good your current results are, if you feel you have the potential to achieve better results, whether that be an improvement in your time management or an improvement in your financial results, then having a growth mindset will be helpful as you read the next chapters.

Light bulbs

Actions

Chapter 6

STRATEGY

1

Prioritise and manage your time

Case Study: **Vivian**

I worked with Vivian, an area leader for a national mid-sized fashion retailer. In her region, Vivian was responsible for seventeen stores across New South Wales. She loved her job, was passionate about her brand and was committed to its success, but she was burnt out and exhausted.

She and I worked together to determine what was causing her to feel burnt out. The answer was that, when she described herself performing her job, what she was describing resembled the description of someone who was working two full-time jobs. Her day job was to visit stores and her evening job was to respond to emails, send updates to her stores and complete KPI reports.

Vivian was working up to fourteen hours a day and recognised that this was not sustainable. It was also not how she wanted to work, because it was impacting her family life and her health. It surprised her to find that working all of those hours did not appear to be improving her results.

Vivian admitted to working the hours she did so she would be perceived as a good area leader. She felt she needed to be visible to all of the staff in her stores and wouldn't leave a store before closing time even though she had mountains of work-related tasks to complete when she got home. She did not want store managers and sales staff to perceive her as not working as hard or as long as they did.

By working so many hours, Vivian was making her role appear unattractive to store managers who might otherwise aspire to step up and become area leaders themselves. She was unintentionally indicating that area leaders needed to work day and night to get the job done. This was a lose/lose situation for everyone.

Traps for area leaders

I have worked with hundreds of area leaders and I have found that there are some common mistakes many area leaders make when it comes to how they spend their time. Some of the common issues I have seen are:

- they overschedule their time and don't allow time for the unexpected
- they are obsessed with spending an unwarranted amount of time in stores
- they don't spend time planning, preparing and establishing key outcomes for each store visit
- they don't prioritise their activities.

Let's now look at each of these in more detail.

Overscheduling and not allowing time for the unexpected

Area leaders can fall into the trap of overscheduling – not allowing time and space to plan and work on their business, or to deal with the unexpected. They can be beyond busy, going from store to store and filling their diaries to an unworkable and unrealistic capacity, causing themselves additional (but avoidable) stress.

Nothing disappoints store managers more than a call from their area leader to say she or he has been held up, or something urgent has cropped up elsewhere and the anticipated store visit needs to be rescheduled.

Obsession with spending unwarranted amounts of time in stores

There is no doubt that area leaders assert the greatest influence when dealing directly with the teams in their stores. But the focus needs to be on the quality of those store visits, not the quantity.

Area leaders can develop a mindset that the more time they spend in stores the better they are doing their jobs and the better the support is that they are providing. There is no evidence supporting this misapprehension that a store's results will be better the more times an area leader visits the store or the longer the visits are. I can recall examples of times when area leaders I was leading took a few weeks of annual leave and, during the time they were on leave, their stores exceeded budget expectations. I believe this was due to those area leaders concentrating, in the time before they were away, on setting expectations for when they would be absent and it was also due to their store managers working together, relying on and supporting each other more during the time their area leader was away.

Actually, visiting a store more than is necessary can be detrimental to the long-term development of a store manager, reducing the need for her or him to develop the ability to problem solve, to make decisions and to improve leadership skills.

Constant visits by area leaders can also cause store managers to lose their belief in themselves and in the fact that they are able to do their jobs effectively.

No planning, preparation or establishment of key outcomes for store visits

If you have not put adequate preparation into planning each of your store visits and are unclear about the outcomes you need to achieve, then you are most likely to be just ticking boxes to appear to have achieved and not actually achieving. If you are going to stores without a plan, or an outcome to be achieved, you are likely to have no impact on the store's ability to achieve the desired outcomes. This will mean that your precious time is being wasted, along with the valuable time of your store managers, and will make following up on any actions and strategies much more difficult.

Failure to prioritise activities

It is important to examine the areas in which you are currently spending your time so you can start to separate and prioritise what is worth doing from what you could be doing less.

Following is an activity that will produce results you might find useful and, possibly, surprising.

I have done this activity with many area leaders, especially those feeling overwhelmed and overworked. When 'keeping too many plates spinning', you might not be conscious of where you are spending your time and, even more importantly, be unable to decide which activities you should make your priority to achieve positive differences in your results. Making an effort to understand where you are spending time can be the catalyst for improving what you focus on and adjusting your priorities.

On the next page is a table entitled 'Listing activities for one week', listing some key activities that an area leader is most likely to do in a typical week (but feel free to add or delete activities to adapt the table so it relates specifically to the way you work).

At the end of each day, for the period of one week, allocate the hours/minutes you spent on each function listed and record the results in the table. This will give you a clear idea of how you are spending your time every day.

At the end of the week, use the 'Prioritising activities' table on the page following the 'Listing activities for one week' table to allocate a number to each activity, from 1 through to 10 (or to 12 if you have added activities of your own in the spaces provided), based on how much time you spent on each activity for the week. The activity to which you allocate number 1 will be the activity on which you spent the most time. Continue to allocate numbers to the activities in the list, 2-10 (or 2-12), in order from greatest to least amount of time spent.

Suppose it is possible to design a plan for exactly how you should spend your time, based on what you believe will have the biggest impact on results. Which activities from the list in the first table do you believe have the greatest impact on sales, and which do not? In the second column of the 'Prioritising activities' table, allocate numbers from 1 through to 10 (or 1 to 12, if you have added activities of your own in the spaces provided), indicating highest priority (aimed at impacting results most) to lowest, with 1 being the highest priority.

LISTING ACTIVITIES FOR ONE WEEK

ACTIVITY	MONDAY	TUESDAY	WEDNESDAY	THURSDAY	FRIDAY	SAT/SUN	TOTAL (h/min)
Planning and preparing for store visits							
Travelling to stores							
Store visits and one-on-ones							
Recruitment/vetting resumes and interviewing							
Reporting/ KPI management							
Meetings with leaders and performing other support/head office functions							
Administration/emails							
Marketing/planning and executing local store activities							
Training/developing leaders							
Meetings with store managers/ assistant store managers							
Other:							
Other:							

This table is available for you to copy from my website: www.alisoncrabb.com.au

PRIORITISING ACTIVITIES		
AREA LEADER ACTIVITIES	**NUMBERS ALLOCATED (FROM 1 to 10 [OR 12]) TO RANK EACH ACTIVITY (1 = most time spent)**	**NUMBERS ALLOCATED TO PRIORITISE ACTIVITIES (1 = greatest impact on results)**
Planning and preparing for store visits		
Travelling to stores		
Store visits and one-on-ones		
Recruitment/vetting resumes and interviewing		
Reporting/KPI management		
Meetings with leaders and performing other support/head office functions		
Administration/emails		
Marketing/planning and executing local store activities		
Training/developing leaders		
Meetings with store managers/assistant store managers		
Other:		
Other:		

This table is available for you to copy from my website: www.alisoncrabb.com.au

From the list in the tables, there are probably not going to be any activities that you can eliminate altogether. However, focusing on quality not quantity and putting more focus and effort into the activities that will help improve your results will ensure better use of your time.

After completing the tables, you will have a full week of data showing you how you actually spend your time and you will be able to reflect on which of your activities will make the biggest difference to your results.

Are you spending too much time on activities that have little or no impact on results?

For example, you might find that you are spending the majority of your time in stores. If so, are your store visits carried out in a way that delivers key outcomes for the business? Are store visits an activity for which you need to spend more time planning and preparing, so you can improve the way in which you conduct your visits to make them more effective?

When you calculate the total time you spend on the road, are you spending a day a week in your car driving from store to store? Sometimes this is unavoidable – but ask yourself if there is a better way to do it.

If you are working long hours, and fear this will become unsustainable, completing the tables and prioritising your activities will help to shed light on the areas in which you are spending most of your time. Your goal should be to use the time more productively to deliver better results.

Based on what you believe to be activities that represent time well spent, what changes do you need to make to how you are spending time so that you are using your time in ways that will best impact your results.

Scheduling your activities

Area leaders all need to be mindful of how they spend their time and prioritise their activities. So let's look at how you schedule your time and see if there is a way to ensure you feel in control and you are investing the right amount of time in the right activities.

Starting with your month, your week and your day, the following are some strategies that might help you.

Your month

It is important to think about your time in whole months, rather than week-to-week, or day-to-day. The following suggestions will help you to schedule your time based around your month.

Whether you have an online diary or a paper diary, I suggest you always start with a monthly planner. I also recommend always having your next month's calendar handy.

There will be key activities that you will have every month and these should be listed ahead of time.

I offer the following suggestions as a guide. The way you adapt them will vary depending on how many stores you oversee, but you can make adjustments according to your specific requirements.

MONTHLY COMMITMENTS

Put into your diary all of the commitments you have for the month, such as store manager meetings, assistant store manager meetings, training or planning sessions that you are either attending or facilitating, area leader meetings, product updates, local store marketing activities, recruitment days, etc. Once you have done this, you will be able to see the number of days you have left for other activities.

The following are some recommendations for prioritising and allocating time in your monthly plan:

- Mondays: administration, leadership calls, planning for the week's store visits
- Tuesdays: store visits
- Wednesdays: store visits
- Thursdays: store visits
- Fridays: keep free for anything that might arise - urgent store visits, meetings, interviews, etc.

Mondays are generally not a good day to visit stores because this is the day when store managers are often out of the stores and Mondays can often be a quieter trading day. For this reason, Monday each week is the best day for you to plan your store visits for the week. Tuesdays, Wednesdays and Thursdays are the best days to make the visits.

Area leaders can fall into the trap of overscheduling themselves and filling their diaries, so I always encourage them to keep Fridays free for the unexpected. This might include important recruitment interviews, dealing with a challenge or issue at a store, or an unexpected unscheduled meeting. If you are lucky enough to avoid any unexpected demands cropping up on your Friday, you can use the day to visit a store that needs additional support, or use the time for follow up or to work with a particular individual or team. I know there is always something to do and creating spare time ahead of when that time might be needed is better than cancelling a pre-arranged store visit to make the necessary free time.

WORKING ON BUSINESS (WOB) DAYS – ONE DAY PER MONTH

Working on business (WOB) days are business planning and reflection days (as opposed to the regular 'working in the business' days of your area leader role dealing with stores). These are days you allocate for looking at your results as a whole. They provide a chance to step back and assess things from a distance.

To do this effectively, I recommend you need one day per month – either on the last day of the month or the first day of the new month, depending on how quickly you can gain access to important KPI reports and results that will provide you with the information to not only see your region's results but to understand how they were achieved, regardless of whether the results were pleasing or disappointing.

Here are some questions to consider that might help you.

- What positive KPI results did your region achieve?
- Which KPIs results were disappointing and what indications of them did you miss?
- How does your staffing look? Are there vacancies you need to fill?
- What leadership positions do you have vacant, if any?
- What is your plan to fill any leadership vacancies?
- Does the filling of vacancies require your focus this month?
- Of which stores/results are you most proud?
- Which specific results do you find disappointing?
- What are some key areas on which you should focus for the new month/season?

Your answers to these questions will help you formulate some of the focus areas for your store visits and store manager meetings for the new month. This process will also indicate the stores and individuals you need to reward and recognise.

I guarantee that investing your time in doing this will pay huge dividends. Not only will you feel more in control of your business, you will have better quality conversations with your teams and will spend more time focusing on the things that matter. This will increase your confidence, enhance your business acumen and improve your results.

Your week

Remember, when planning each week, I recommend that Mondays are for working *on* your business and planning your store visits for the week, while Fridays should be kept free for the unexpected. So, this leaves you three days for store visits.

When it comes to planning your schedule of store visits, Chapters 7 and 8 focus on how to schedule, plan, prepare and execute great store visits.

Your day

Based on the monthly and weekly schedules already described, most weeks you will have three days for store visits. This thought might make you anxious because you could be accustomed to spending most of your time visiting stores - perhaps as many as four or five days per week.

When you have learnt to plan, prepare and execute efficient and successful visits you will see that it is the quality of the visits and not the quantity that makes the biggest difference to your results.

Depending on your store locations, I recommend you visit one store per day, or no more than two stores on any one day.

Once you learn to take control and strategically think about how to schedule your time, you will start to see benefits quickly. You will be able to think more clearly, be more outcome focused and will not feel as though you are constantly rushing from place to place.

Light bulbs

Actions

Chapter 7

STRATEGY
2

Maximise your store visits

Case Study: **Helen**

I worked with Helen, an area leader for a mid-sized national retailer. Although Helen was based in Western Australia and was responsible for eight stores there, she was also responsible for five stores in South Australia.

I asked her about the results from each of the two states. What fascinated me was that Helen's South Australian stores were significantly outperforming the Western Australian stores, even though she was responsible for more stores in Western Australia. Sales were higher in South Australia, staff retention was better and there seemed to be far fewer issues with which to deal generally.

As we spoke in more depth, I asked Helen a lot of questions so she could reflect and identify why there might be such a difference in results and, more importantly, what was creating that difference. I was interested to know how she was leading her Western Australian stores compared to her South Australian stores. Below is a brief outline of her feedback on each of the states.

Western Australia

Being based in Western Australia it was easy for Helen to visit the stores regularly. She visited each store at least once a week; usually visiting two stores on most days. Her greatest frustration was feeling that she was constantly running from store to store, 'putting out fires' and spending a great deal of time dealing with people problems.

It was a struggle to keep staff for long, so Helen was also spending a great deal of time recruiting new team members.

The Western Australian store managers didn't meet as a group because Helen believed this would mean they were spending valuable time out of stores. She felt such meetings were unnecessary, as well as costly. She tended to work with each store manager individually and made sure she was always close by, in case they needed her. Store managers seemed to be reliant on Helen to make decisions.

South Australia

Helen could only visit her South Australian stores every eight weeks, so she had to lead these stores a little differently from her Western Australian stores. When she was in South Australia it could only be for a few days at a time.

When Helen arrived in South Australia, she would gather all of the store managers together for a team meeting, because this seemed an efficient way of making the most of her time while she was there. She would give the managers a business update and confirm sales targets for the next two months. They would then discuss results and share ideas and strategies.

The South Australian store managers were a cohesive group of leaders. They worked together and contacted each other regularly to solve problems. They would only contact Helen when they were in need of her expertise and advice. The South Australian store managers seemed to have taken more ownership of their stores than their Western Australian counterparts. They were a tightknit connected leadership group who nearly always achieved their budget goals and had very high retention of team members.

'Light bulbs' appeared, for me and for Helen, as she recounted the differences between the ways in which she led the two states. She began to see that what she had unintentionally created for herself in Western Australia was a leadership style that made her store managers reliant on her. She didn't value the time she spent in Western Australia as much, because she knew she would be back again the following week or could pop into a store at a moment's notice. The Western Australian store managers didn't need to think for themselves and solve their own challenges, and Helen hadn't built the same tightknit community of leaders that she had in South Australia.

Visiting stores as often as Helen did in Western Australia doesn't teach store managers to step up, take responsibility, solve their own problems and deliver results. It doesn't allow them to be true business leaders.

To improve results, it is imperative that everyone in a leadership role needs to step up and this starts with area leaders. Area leaders need to provide appropriate levels of support, set clear expectations, manage those expectations and create the space in which store managers can step up and do their jobs.

It creates a lose/lose situation if area leaders try to be the pseudo store managers of multiple stores, leaving store managers to be nothing more than store caretakers. It results in a lack of ownership of stores and of results by store managers and staff, which leads to frustration. It just doesn't work!

The best results occur when store managers are allowed to develop into true business leaders, taking spiritual and psychological ownership of their stores, caring about their staff, caring about their customers and caring about their results.

To assist you in improving the outcomes of your store visits and the results they achieve, complete the 'Store visit maintenance checklist' on the following pages. It is a kind of 'health check' aimed at helping you to evaluate what you are doing well and the changes you may need to consider making to improve your results.

After completing the checklist, you will easily see which strategies you marked 'Yes' and which you marked 'No'.

Some of the strategies that you are not implementing, and you marked 'No', may not be important to you right now but, as you continue to read through this book, I hope you will see that you may want to consider also implementing some of those strategies in your region.

Store visit maintenance checklist

Read through the behaviours listed in the checklist on the following pages.

- If you always behave in the manner described, circle 'Y' for 'Yes'.
- If you behave in the manner described only some of the time, circle 'S' for 'Sometimes'.
- If you never behave in the manner described, circle 'N' for 'No'.

Try to avoid circling 'S' for 'Sometimes' unless it proves really difficult to decide between 'Y' for 'Yes' and 'N' for 'No' because this response, while indicating room for improvement, does make it difficult to determine the behaviours on which you need to focus most to improve what is achieved by your store visits.

STORE VISIT MAINTENANCE CHECKLIST			
I look at the results and key performance indicators (KPIs) of each of my stores, so that I know exactly how each store is performing and can note opportunities for improvement.	Y	S	N
My shop visits are always well prepared. I know the areas on which I need to focus with each store manager to make the most out of each visit.	Y	S	N
I have a monthly meeting with all my store managers together and use this for communication, focus and development.	Y	S	N
I follow up on strategies from the store manager meetings with each store manager during store visits.	Y	S	N
I have a template that I follow for each store visit. This assists me in being consistent and staying on track to help achieve my outcomes and follow up on previous visits.	Y	S	N
I use store visits to communicate important information about various areas of the business, such as products, marketing and merchandising.	Y	S	N
I use store visits to build trusting relationships with the store manager and the in-store team.	Y	S	N
I work to build relationships with assistant store managers so that I can assist with their development and career goals.	Y	S	N
I spend time getting to know all of the staff, regardless of their roles, so I can understand what is important to them and am aware of their aspirations.	Y	S	N

I finish each store visit by working with the store manager to put together her/his action plan, focusing on no more than two or three objectives and the ways these can be met.	Y	S	N
I create time in my schedule to follow up on each store manager's progress with her/his action plan.	Y	S	N
I have a strategic approach to how I schedule visits, so I can spend most time where it is needed.	Y	S	N
I am comfortable with conversing honestly with staff to help them improve in their roles.	Y	S	N
I give praise and recognition to acknowledge achievement of great results.	Y	S	N

This 'Store visit maintenance checklist' is available for you to copy from my website: www.alisoncrabb.com.au

Light bulbs

Actions

Chapter 8

STRATEGY
3

Deliver on your store visits

Case Study: **Mike**

I worked with Mike, an area leader who oversaw a large region of sixteen stores. Geographically, most of his stores were close together which made it easy for him to travel to all of his stores regularly.

Each week Mike was on a mission to visit as many stores as possible. He judged the success of his week by how many stores he had been able to visit. In a typical month, he would be able to visit each of his stores two or three times and, the more often he visited a store, the better he felt.

As we started to work together, he displayed frustration that his stores were not achieving their budget goals even though he was providing a lot of support and being very visible within his region.

Mike was frustrated that store managers were not taking responsibility for their results or finding ways to achieve their sales budgets themselves. The pressure to deliver results was weighing heavily on him. He was often being questioned by his general manager about why his stores were not meeting expectations and what he was doing about it - which only amplified his desire to spend more of his time in stores.

I asked Mike some questions about how he saw his role and how he was working to understand what could be contributing to his disappointing results. When I asked him why he felt it necessary to visit his stores so frequently, he replied, 'It's what I have always done.'

He was right, it was what he had always done, but there was no real logic or strategy behind why he visited his stores so regularly - especially when it was not delivering results.

Many underachieving area leaders over the years have given me numerous reasons why they felt the need to visit stores frequently, even though it did not seem to improve their results. Among those reasons I have consistently heard, 'So that stores feel I am supporting them,' or, 'I need to make sure they are doing the things they are meant to be doing.'

I began to wonder how area leaders making so many store visits impacts on the mindset of their store managers.

If I was a store manager and my own area leader felt the need to visit my store so often I would ask myself, 'Why does she/he not trust me?' Or worse, when faced with a solvable problem, I might reach the point of saying to myself, 'I have a problem that I need to solve, but I will wait for my area leader to visit and solve it for me.' Area leaders who visit stores more often than necessary tend to take initiative away from store managers to control situations and solve their own problems. Store managers develop the mindset of 'caretakers' rather than of leaders in the business. They feel like they are just in their roles to manage the status quo and make sure their stores are open, while all the big decisions are to be made by someone else. Handing over responsibility in this way, so area leaders make the decisions and solve the problems, creates in store managers a lack of ownership and a lack of accountability for their results.

I have often been asked, 'How many stores should an area leader have in their region?' This is a difficult question to answer because the ideal number depends on a lot of factors, such as the geography of the area (regional or metropolitan), the size of the stores and the specific requirements and responsibilities of the area leader. However, I am convinced that area leaders can be responsible for larger regions with greater numbers of stores if they implement the strategies suggested in this book, becoming more strategic in their approach and the way they spend their time and providing the space and opportunity for store managers to step up. There also needs to be a commitment from the business leaders to provide training and development to store managers, providing them with the necessary skills.

Have you ever:

* asked yourself, while driving to a store for a store visit, 'What will I cover in this visit today?' – being unclear on the outcomes you wanted to achieve?

- left a store after a store visit and remembered later that there was something you intended to share or discuss, but that you had forgotten?
- been unexpectedly 'blindsided' by a resignation from one of your store managers?
- carried out activities in a store that are really the role of the store manager?
- needed to reschedule a store visit at the last minute to 'put out a fire' in a store somewhere else?

All of these scenarios can result from a lack of planning and a lack of preparation for your store visits. They can all be avoided with some focus on the right areas.

The following pages contain some of my recommended strategies to assist with preparation and planning. Some of these strategies involve a change of belief and mindset while some will require a change in behaviour. They might be enough to encourage some area leaders to undertake a degree of self-reflection and self-discipline, to change what isn't working and try something new.

Strategies for store visits

Quality not quantity of store visits

In most cases, you should only need to visit a particular store once or twice a month – at most!

It is the quality of a store visit rather than the quantity of store visits that will make the biggest difference to your results. The need to visit stores too frequently can sometimes result from lack of preparation.

If every store visit was prepared and delivered with purposeful outcomes, area leaders wouldn't need to spend quite so much precious time on the road driving from store to store. Their time could be spent on important areas of the business and would contribute more to favourable results.

Creating business folders

Do you keep a notebook and make notes during each store visit? When conducting store visits, how do you make notes regarding your conversations? What system do you have in place for following up after your store visits?

I have found that area leaders use a variety of tools to varying degrees of success. The following is what I have taught many area leaders and it has changed the way many of them work.

I own the fact that what I am about to suggest isn't the most environmentally-friendly system and there are more ecofriendly ways to store information. But, using a pen and paper (and relaxing your environmentally responsible attitudes in this one instance) may be a sacrifice worth making for an enormous difference to your results and the way you work.

This system will enable you to have more focused store visits and to keep all of your information in the one place. It will also make it easier to follow up whether staff have enacted suggestions made during your visit.

I suggest you purchase two good quality display books for each store in your region. If there are ten stores you will buy twenty folders. Invest in the ones that have twenty plastic pockets in which you can insert documents and that allow you to insert a page into the front cover. These should each cost you $7.00, or less, from major stationery suppliers.

I call these 'business folders'. For each store, one of the business folders you purchase is for you and the other is for the store manager. Each business folder becomes the place for all of the information you gather about one store to be filed. Information, such as the store budget, the store business plan, local store marketing plans, notes from one-on-ones and any other business information should be kept in a store's business folder.

This means that you have one folder for each store and each store manager also has her/his own folder. Each store manager should use her/his business folder for the same purpose as you use your folder; to store all the business information pertaining to the store.

In addition, I suggest purchasing two A4 exercise books for each store. Again, this is one book per store for you and one for each of the store managers. The book for each store should be kept in your business folder for that store. These books are where you make notes from store visits, from discussions with store managers and assistant store managers, and from one-on-ones with staff, along with any other notes you might make relating to individual stores.

When you conduct your store visits, you and the store manager should both use your business folder for reference and to make further notes.

Use of these folders creates a more professional business mindset, not only for an area leader but also for store managers, and it makes following up much easier for you.

Scheduling your store visits

The way you schedule your store visits does require some thought. There are a number of ways to plan your schedule.

Store visits are often scheduled with the main consideration being geography and proximity, which makes sense if your goal is to spend the least time driving from store to store. But it would be more effective and efficient to schedule your visits based on where you are needed most.

How you schedule your store visits should be determined by the specific situation of each of your stores, such as the level of experience of the store manager, the level of experience of the in-store team and the store's recent results. New stores can sometimes require more of your focus than established stores.

The location of the stores (regional or metropolitan) will also determine how you schedule your visits. Visits to regional stores sometimes need to be scheduled based on geography if the visits require significant time on the road. Regional stores often receive fewer visits due to their location, which means those visits require even more time and planning so you make the most of your time when you are there.

What I have found works best is to start by prioritising stores into categories A, B and C, as described under the headings on the next page.

PRIORITY A STORES

Priority A stores require a high level of support for a variety of reasons, which may include the following.

- The store might have a new store manager.
- The store might have a manager that isn't performing to expectations.
- The store temporarily might not have a store manager.
- The store might be a new store that has recently opened.

PRIORITY B STORES

Priority B stores require less support than Priority A stores. These are the stores that:

- have a good level of leadership experience
- maintain very good results
- perform to expectations
- have a settled team.

PRIORITY C STORES

Priority C stores perform very well. They are usually your 'blue chip' stores. They will:

- often be located in major shopping centres
- have managers with a high level of leadership experience
- be able to maintain or exceed expectations
- be busy stores, usually trading seven days per week.

I find that categorising stores according to the criteria above works very well. From your own experience, you might wish to add some of your own criteria to these lists as well.

You know best what level of support each of your stores requires, so you should be well-equipped to allocate your stores to A, B or C priority.

Spend some time considering the stores you oversee then, based on the criteria I have just provided for Priority A, Priority B and Priority C stores, list each of them in the appropriate column of the table below.

PRIORITY A STORES	PRIORITY B STORES	PRIORITY C STORES

This table is available for you to copy from my website: www.alisoncrabb.com.au

Scheduling your store visits for the month

Once you have listed your stores and they each have been assigned a priority, plan your store visits for the month, in the following order.

1. Priority A stores
2. Priority B stores
3. Priority A stores (again)
4. Priority C stores

Naturally, you will schedule your Priority A stores as your first visits for the month. These visits will be at the start of the month, which is a great time to set the stores' daily, weekly and monthly goals and ensure they have a plan in place with which you can assist and that you are able to follow up.

Priority B stores will be next. It is likely that your visits to these stores will be mid-month (depending on the number of Priority A stores you need to visit). Remember, these stores are generally solid performers.

You will then return to your Priority A stores for a follow-up visit to check on their progress and assist with implementing the plan put in place at the beginning of the month.

Your visits to your Priority C stores will be later in the month. Remember, your Priority C stores are your best performing stores, so visiting them later in the month means you will usually have an opportunity to acknowledge their positive results for the month.

Following the schedule just described means that you will spend more time in the stores that require more support and you will be using your time where it is most needed.

I have been asked whether visiting the Priority C stores towards the end of every month created a belief in the minds of the store managers that their stores were not as important as the stores I visited earlier and at which I spent more time. It is important, to avoid this misconception, to communicate to the store managers and staff of your Priority C stores that you visit them later in the month because you have absolute confidence and trust in them and just want to empower them to get on with the job they are doing.

Each month, you should spend time reassessing and reprioritising your stores. A lot can change from month to month, so a store that is a Priority C store this month could easily become a Priority A store in the following months.

I am surprised to hear that some area leaders don't always let the store managers know when they are going to visit their stores. When I ask why, I am usually told it is in order to surprise the store managers so that the area leaders can see what is 'really' going on in stores, or else these area leaders don't like to work to a schedule in case unexpected things crop up and they can't get to a store as planned.

It is almost impossible for a store visit to be effective and purposeful if the store manager isn't aware of it beforehand and is, therefore, unprepared.

Once you have scheduled your visits, it is important that you communicate the schedule to all of your store managers and their teams. This will ensure that your store managers can prepare for your visit and they will usually have the store looking fabulous because they want to impress you.

It also means that the store can be adequately staffed in advance so you will be able to spend quality time with the store manager and members of the in-store team.

Preparing for your store visits

The saying that 'Time is money' is certainly true when it comes to store visits. Area leaders spend up to 80% of their time conducting store visits, so it makes sense that, if you want to improve your results, preparing yourself efficiently for your store visits is essential.

Following the suggestions I have made will require a bigger focus on your preparation for store visits and will require you to have a clear purpose and a clear idea of the outcomes you want to be achieved. It is often our mindset that needs addressing and changing first when it comes to the discipline of spending time on preparation.

If your store managers are made aware you will be visiting, they can also prepare so the most is made of the time you spend with them.

As you start to prepare using some of the strategies I have described, ask yourself:

- 'What are my region's profit or sales targets for the month?'
- 'How much is each of my stores contributing to my overall target for the region?'

If you have a sales target of $500,000 for the month and one of your stores has a target of $50,000, that store visit is worth 10% of your overall monthly target. When you can interpret each of your store visits in this way, it will help to change your mindset, the way in which you prepare and how much value you place on each visit.

Here are some key areas on which to focus when preparing for each store visit.

- Look at the store's KPIs.

- Store manager preparation.

- Managing brand standards.

These areas of focus will now be discussed in more detail.

LOOK AT EACH STORE'S KPIS

I have always said that 'KPIs don't lie'. Performance indicators will tell the story of what is going on in your region and in each of your stores. The better you can get to know these numbers, the better you can implement specific strategies to improve results.

The key performance indicator (KPI) template

I recommend designing a standard KPI template that you can use in your preparation for each store visit. If you are part of a team of area leaders, this might be something you can create together.

Whenever I am working with area leaders, whether it be one-on-one or with a whole group of area leaders together, we spend time designing a KPI template specific to each of their businesses. This makes an enormous difference to the quality of store visits and the business acumen of area leaders.

Once you have designed your own template, you can amend it and perfect it as you become more comfortable using it.

Your KPI template might include such KPIs as:

- sales – last year's figures, figures to date for the current year and forecasts for the rest of the current year

- margins – last year's figures, figures to date for the current year and forecasts for the rest of the current year

- costs – last year's figures, figures to date for the current year and forecasts for the rest of the current year

- customer reports

- staff reports.

Whatever the measures recorded for your business, take the time to familiarise yourself with the details, so you know the numbers.

I always preferred to handwrite the KPIs of each of my stores on my template. I am not a fan of fancy systems and spreadsheet software that will populate tables of figures for you because this inhibits your ability to develop your business acumen. Handwriting the numbers helps to teach you the key drivers of your business and improves your business acumen and understanding, which is essential for your growth in your role.

Each store is unique and needs to be treated differently (remember the Priority A, B and C stores). It is likely that there will be a slightly different focus for each of your stores. For example, busy shopping centre stores might have a greater need to focus on achieving high volumes of sales and high volumes of customers, while community strip stores might have a greater need to focus on marketing and higher sales per customer.

Staffing levels and rosters are a key focus for most retailers and each of your stores will have different staffing requirements. Therefore, designing a standard KPI template to help you assess how each store is tracking and what each store needs will help you to have clear and focused store visits.

Store visit preparation sheet

Once you have a clear impression of each store and its results, you need to ask yourself:

- 'What do I want to achieve from visiting this store?'
- 'What do I need to walk away from the store visit having achieved?'
- 'What do I need the store manager to know/achieve?'

To help with achieving your desired outcomes, I recommend you design a 'Store visit preparation' template to help you prepare to cover everything you want to cover during the store visit. This template for the store visit will help you stay on track and ensure you are thorough in your approach, so you cover everything required.

I preferred to spend time on Mondays completing the templates for my week of visits ahead and planning the visits for the week.

On the next page is a sample template you might like to use as a guide for designing your own.

STORE VISIT PREPARATION SHEET	
Store:	**Date of visit:**
What are the specific outcomes I want to achieve from this store visit?	
What are the key strategies to follow up from the store managers' meeting?	
What are the KPIs telling me about this store's results? Which KPIs need my focus?	
What specific reports will I need for reference? Is there any additional preparation I need to do?	
Are there any specific questions I need to ask to help me achieve my desired outcomes?	
Who else in the store do I need to speak to/connect with?	
How/when will I follow up to ensure desired outcomes are achieved?	

This table is available for you to copy from my **website:** www.alisoncrabb.com.au

STORE MANAGER PREPARATION

I am passionate about everyone in retail stepping up, or 'levelling up' – to put it in video gaming parlance. By this I mean to progress to the next level. For this to happen area leaders need to do their jobs and allow store managers to do theirs and grow in their roles.

It is important that the two roles of area leader and store manager are not confused. Often I see area leaders taking on some of the responsibilities of store managers which, as I described earlier, can become a source of frustration for the area leaders and often leaves the store managers feeling more like caretakers and less like leaders.

If we want our store managers to improve their business acumen and to take more ownership of their results, this starts with teaching them what the key drivers of their business are and with being transparent in regard to their results. We need to allow store managers to feel like true business leaders, having ownership of their results and the ability to personally impact them.

I recommend that you create another template for each store manager to complete prior to your visit to her/his store. This template should include somewhere for store managers to record the KPIs for their stores as well as questions to consider about their businesses.

Each store manager should complete their preparation sheet prior to your visit so they are clear about what they hope to achieve from your visit.

STORE MANAGER PREPARATION SHEET	
Store:	**Date of visit:**
What specific outcomes do I want to achieve from my time with my area leader?	
How are my individual team members performing? Is there anything regarding team performance that I need to discuss with my area leader?	
What are the KPIs telling me about my store's results? Which KPIs need my focus? What specific reports will I need to show my area leader? Is there any additional preparation I need to do?	
Are there specific questions I need to ask or support I need to request to help me achieve my desired outcomes?	
From a leadership perspective, is there anything with which I need support?	
How/when will I follow up to ensure outcomes are achieved?	

This table is available for you to copy from my website: www.alisoncrabb.com.au

MANAGING BRAND STANDARDS

Retailers take pride in their brand. The brand is the way customers recognise and experience the business. It can include marketing material, advertising, a logo, the way staff presents to customers, and the appearance of shopfronts and retail premises. The way merchandise is displayed is a large part of this. In-season stock needs to be displayed in a prominent place and stores need to be generally well presented.

It is the area leader's responsibility to ensure that stores meet brand requirements, but it is the store manager's responsibility to ensure the ongoing upholding and maintenance of brand standards.

Many retailers have their own brand standards checklist. If this has not been devised and is not in place, I recommend that a brand standards checklist be designed based on the brand standards of the business. This checklist should be completed by the store manager prior to the area leader's visit so that the area leader can sign off on it if the store fulfils all the requirements, or can take care of anything that needs addressing if it doesn't.

This will mean the store manager takes responsibility for meeting brand standards and it will save you time during your visit.

Tools for your visit

If you have followed the suggestions I have made, you will now have:

1. a key performance indicators (KPIs) template
2. a store visit preparation sheet
3. a business folder for each store.

Each store manager will also have:

1. a store manager preparation sheet
2. a brand standards checklist
3. a business folder for her/his own store.

If you design and utilise these tools, you will improve the quality of your store visits and the outcomes achieved by them.

Have a consistent focus

It is important not to focus on too many strategies at once.

Your store manager meeting, held at the start of each month, should be the vehicle to drive the strategy for your region (see Chapter 10). On your store visits, you can then follow up on the discussion and decisions from the meeting, helping and supporting store managers with their implementation of the strategy.

When you have a well thought out, well-planned monthly store manager meeting, your store visits are able to reflect and reinforce the focus from the meeting and any key strategies moving forward.

If your store manager meeting highlighted an upcoming promotion, that should be followed up during your store visit.

Executing your store visits

Once you have done the planning, it is time to visit your stores.

The goal is for your visits to be well-planned and well-prepared, so that you don't need to visit every store often. Preparation and planning will mean that you will spend more quality time in each store and each visit will usually take half the day, or a maximum of three hours.

I prefer for one-on-ones with store managers to take place away from the store. A local coffee shop is usually a good place to sit and focus, with no distractions.

Store managers appreciate receiving individual attention and this helps build strong trusting relationships with them.

I understand that, due to staffing levels, off-site meetings of this kind might present a challenge but, if the visit is planned well in advance, plenty of notice is given and the visits occur infrequently, staffing levels should be able to be addressed to accommodate your visit.

On the day you are planning to visit staffing levels might be inadequate, meaning that the staff with whom you want to meet are not free. I suggest that you organise visits on a day when staffing levels are not an issue. It is pointless visiting a store if you can't spend quality uninterrupted time with the store manager, or with anyone else with whom you want a one-on-one discussion.

Importantly, part of your store visit should also be devoted to spending time with the assistant store manager. This meeting should be an abridged version of your discussion with the store manager. Meeting in this way with assistant store managers will help you to build relationships with them and provide one-on-one support for their development as future leaders.

If there is part-time or casual staff working on the day of your visit, ensure you spend time with them also – ideally, out of the store, but even time within the store would suffice.

Conducting your one-on-ones

Your one-on-one discussions with your store managers are possibly the best opportunity you will have to ensure the agreed strategies to improve your region's results are being implemented. Remember, your goal should be to elevate the quality of your one-on-ones so that the need for you to visit stores frequently is reduced. Having positive and focused one-on-ones is also the best way to build trusting relationships with your store managers and with all staff members.

Here are some tips to help you with the effectiveness of your one-on-ones.

AVOID ANY INTERRUPTIONS

Be genuinely interested and attentive during one-on-ones with store managers. Just as you have spent time preparing for the discussion, so have they.

Your mindset for any one-on-ones, with store managers or staff, needs to be the same as your mindset would be for a business meeting. This means putting away your mobile phone or, if you must keep it near you, turning the ringtone down and avoiding answering any calls, if you can. Your store managers will really appreciate having your undivided attention.

As much as we might want to get to know our staff, it is important that the time spent together in one-on-one discussions is meaningful and businesslike. Don't be distracted by fluffy conversation about your dog, or what you watched on television the previous night. This is just a waste of valuable time. I like to save this kind of informal chit chat for when I first arrive in a store and greet the team, or as we are walking to the coffee shop for a one-on-one.

BE CLEAR OF PURPOSE

Once we sit to begin our discussion, I like to start by stating what I hope to achieve from our discussion time together. At the beginning of the discussion, I always ask the store manager or staff member what they hope to achieve from it too.

Remember, any one-on-one is a two-way conversation and you need to ensure that, as well as your desired outcomes for the meeting being achieved, the desired outcomes of the individual with whom you are meeting are also achieved.

I always had a template for my one-on-ones. This helped me stay on track and ensured I didn't leave the store after the visit having forgotten to discuss something that I needed to cover. While having a template does help you keep on track, it is important to be mindful that you also ensure that your one-on-ones don't feel like interviews or interrogations.

On the next page is a sample template that you can use for your one-on-ones or that might be helpful in assisting you to design your own.

I like to use paper and pen to make my notes because I find devices like iPads impersonal and distracting. Just remember that the store manager will have done preparation for your store visit and, like you, should have a business folder containing information and topics for discussion (see where business folders are discussed earlier in this chapter).

From a single discussion, I usually restrict the number of actions or strategies we record and plan to implement to just two or three. One strategy, well implemented, can sometimes be better than three which have not been carried out well.

Simply use my recommendation of limiting the number of activities and strategies to be carried out as a result of each discussion as a guide and base your own expectations on each store's results and the level of experience of each store manager. Based on the discussion, the area leader and store manager might both have actions to follow up, but I have known some area leaders to have a very long 'To do' list at the end of a visit. This is not what is intended. The purpose of one-on-one discussions of this kind is to empower the store manager to run the store, with your support. Be careful that you do not fall into the habit of stepping in as pseudo store manager and taking over the role.

AREA LEADER STORE VISIT TEMPLATE

Date of visit: **Store:**   **Store manager:**

What I want to achieve from this visit:

What the store manager wants to achieve from this visit:

Review performance/results (what the numbers are saying)
Week to date:

Month to date:

Which KPIs need focus?

People check
Is there anything particular with which the store manager needs help?

How are the individual team members performing? Is there anything we need to discuss in regard to this?

Strategies and actions:
1

2

3

Specific focus:

How/when will I follow up to ensure desired outcomes are achieved?

This table is available for you to copy from my website: www.alisoncrabb.com.au

I have found one-on-ones can cover a range of things that can't always be listed or recorded on a template. However, if you are able to use the template provided on the previous page as a guide and adapt it to your own purposes, it will make a difference to the quality of your store visits.

Following up your store visits

Every store visit should finish with agreement on the strategies or actions to be implemented before the next visit. The store manager will have actions to perform and strategies to implement, but you may also have things that you have agreed to implement or follow up and it is important that you follow through with those. Failure to do this is one certain way to break trust with store managers and staff.

You may agree with your store managers on different ways to follow up on their progress, depending on whether the store you are visiting is a Priority A, Priority B or Priority C store.

You may prefer to allocate time each week for following up or you might make an agreed time at the end of each future visit to do that. If you use a template during each store visit for recording actions and strategies to be implemented, it will make follow up much easier. Sometimes, depending on the nature of the strategies, you will follow up throughout the month via phone or email, rather than waiting until your next store visit.

Regardless of whether you follow up throughout the month or not, it is important that you discuss the strategies decided on the previous visit when you next visit the store. This will help with consistency.

Once you are in the habit of documenting and following up, and encouraging your store managers to do the same, you will see an elevated level of ownership from the store managers for the business and their results.

Light bulbs

Actions

Chapter 9

STRATEGY 4

Engage your part-time workforce

Part-time and casual staff make up almost 70% of the retail workforce. After hospitality, this is the second highest participation rate by part-timers and casual workers in any Australian business sector. Retail is also the biggest area of growth within the female workforce. The employment of casual and part-time staff allows retailers flexibility to have more staff working at peak shopping times and during peak shopping periods.

The availability of casual and part-time work in the retail sector also allows many people to have a role in the workforce while studying or raising a family. Not only employers need flexibility! When handled well, the employment of part-time and casual staff can result in win/win situations, mutually benefitting both retailers and their workforce.

Having such a large part-time and casual workforce, it makes good business sense for retail employers to take good care of them, especially if their products require confident sales staff with good product knowledge. Training new staff can be time-consuming and costly.

I believe retailers could focus and do better in their dealings with part-time and casual employees. I have interviewed many casual workers, be they working parents, students working while studying, or people working casually in a second job. Consistently, I hear that their experience is one of not feeling valued or of feeling like a number or a 'dollar per hour' commodity. Many of them have experienced having shifts cut at the last minute, being asked to come in and cover a shift's staff shortage with little or no notice, being rostered for a four-hour shift only to be sent home early, or being given only a couple of shifts a week which doesn't provide them with an adequate income.

Casual members of staff do not receive the same benefits as full-time employees. They are often excluded from the benefits of store discounts and from opportunities for personal and professional development. What casual staff and part-time staff members really want is to feel valued, appreciated and cared about.

Understanding the make-up of your workforce

This activity is aimed at helping you to determine the type of staff working for you (full-time, part-time or casual) and the percentage of each that make up your total workforce. Fill in the table and perform the calculations to assist you to understand what kinds of workers constitute your workforce.

	BREAKDOWN OF TYPES OF STAFF	
	HEAD COUNT (NOT FTE)*	% OF TOTAL STAFF
TOTAL STAFF NUMBERS		100%
NUMBER OF FULL-TIME STAFF		
NUMBER OF PART-TIME STAFF		
NUMBER OF CASUAL STAFF		

* FTE = Full time equivalent

This table is available for you to copy from my website: www.alisoncrabb.com.au

If casual and part-time staff make up a large percentage of your workforce, the longer they continue working for you the more beneficial it can be for you. The longer these people are employed in your organisation, the better their product knowledge and systems knowledge will be, they will form deeper relationships with staff and customers, and will develop more brand loyalty.

There is a danger for retailers if their part-time and casual staff members do not feel valued, appreciated or cared about because this impacts their desire to go above and beyond for the customer and the brand, or to volunteer more of their effort willingly.

Engaging your casual and part-time workforce

Below are some questions that you might find useful for deciding ways in which you can retain and engage your casual and part-time workers – who probably represent the largest category of workers in your stores!

1   How can you ensure these workers are part of the community within your region?

2   How can you ensure you have very good communication channels with them?

3   How can you gather valuable feedback from these workers?

4   How can you ensure you know their career aspirations?

5   How can you find ways for them to transition from part-time to full-time, and back to part-time, if necessary?

The more you can show genuine appreciation, support and care, understanding their goals and displaying a truly collaborative approach, your casual and part-time workforce will become more committed and will care more about your customers and your results. They will embrace striving for sales targets together with you.

I cannot stress enough that this relationship needs to be built on mutual respect, care and trust. British business magnate, investor and author Richard Branson has been widely quoted as saying the following, which I believe sums it up perfectly:

> *I have always believed that the way you treat your employees is the way they will treat your customers, and that people flourish when they are praised.*

Light bulbs

Actions

Chapter 10

STRATEGY 5

Have meetings that matter

Communication

If you have ever baked a cake, you will be familiar with most recipes instructing you to sift all of the dry ingredients together through a sieve to combine them thoroughly and get rid of the unpleasant lumpy bits. Whether the recipe requires flour, castor sugar, salt, baking powder, baking soda, cocoa or other dry powdered ingredients, all of those ingredients are placed into the top of the sieve, are sifted together and combined to fall lightly and effortlessly through the sieve.

When it comes to communication within an organisation, I see the role of the area leader as equivalent to the part played by the sieve when baking.

Merchandising

Marketing   Technology

Product   Finance

Area leader

Store managers

Area leaders are responsible for ensuring all of the important information from various parts of the business and support functions, such as marketing, merchandising, product, technology and finance, are sifted together and reach the store managers so that they are all informed. Being the organisation's sieves means area leaders need to understand the responsibility they have to their store managers to ensure they pass on to them all the information they need to know while filtering out the 'lumpy bits'. The 'lumpy bits' that are left behind and not filtered through to the store managers will be those pieces of information that may not be necessary or appropriate for them to know (for example, highly sensitive information).

The role of area leader requires you to lead with influence, so the way you communicate to get the right information to the right people at the right time is crucial. Area leaders are the most important cogs in the organisation's wheel. They are the people in a leadership role who have the most contact with stores and, often, have the most influence.

Changes to products and systems and implementation of those changes will be a significant part of your role and, if you do that well, managing expectations and seamlessly implementing new systems, you will save yourself a lot of time that would otherwise be spent putting out spot fires and solving problems.

The sieve system from area leaders to store managers should also operate in the other direction, from area leaders to those providing support and business functions for the stores. Area leaders need to provide important feedback from their stores to their own leadership, combining and communicating information from the stores that will assist with evaluation of current strategies and formulation of possible future strategies.

Store visits will always provide the best vehicle for you to communicate with the store manager and in-store team members (see Chapter 8), however, there are other opportunities for the people of your region to connect and communicate.

If you want to keep all of your staff engaged and updated regarding important information affecting the business, store managers need to fully appreciate the important role they play when it comes to communication.

There should also be an expectation that the sieve model, from area leader to store manager, continues so the information is sifted down the chain again, from the store manager to the rest of the in-store team – so that everyone in the business receives and understands all the important information. This could be achieved by store managers having daily team updates.

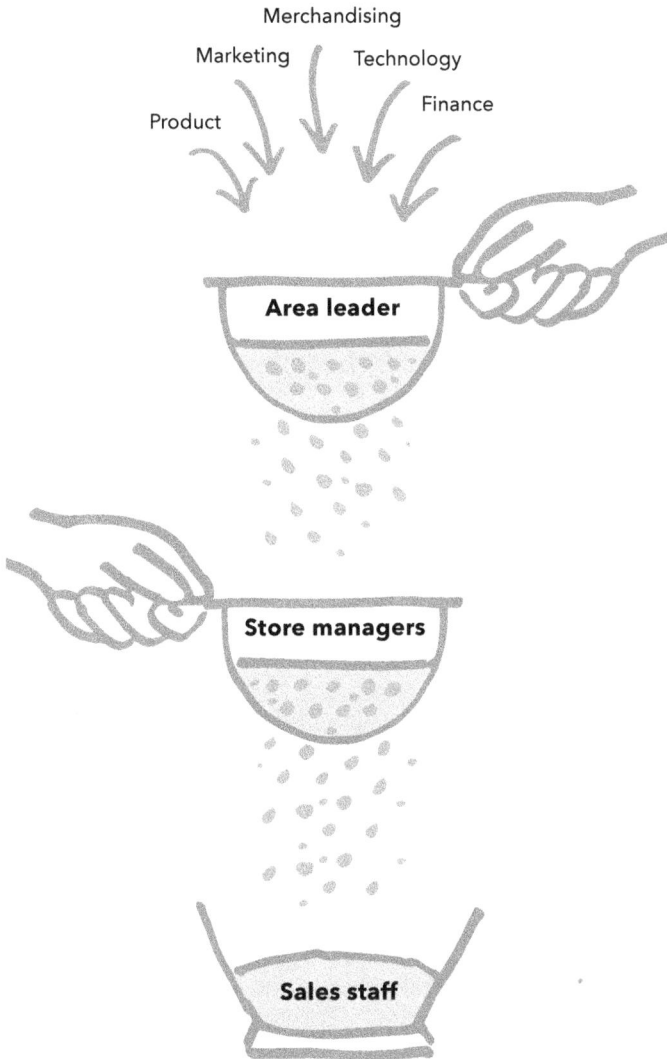

Meetings that matter

Store manager meetings

Case Study: Neil

I worked with Neil, an area leader who was responsible for eleven retail stores. Neil and his fellow area leaders had been holding monthly store manager meetings. However, when the focus of the business began to be to reduce unnecessary costs, store manager meetings were seen as representing one of those unnecessary costs and the decision was made to schedule only quarterly store manager meetings.

As a result of this change, there was a noticeable difference in the level of connection and sense of community felt across Neil's region. It impacted his ability to communicate important information to the stores. If any store manager missed one meeting, this meant that she or he would not see the other store managers for six months. Support for each other waned and so did their results.

Neil believed that the most significant impact on his results had been caused by the change from monthly to quarterly store manager meetings. He was supported in this belief by his store managers and by area leaders from other regions. As a result, Neil's region, along with those of his peers, reverted to holding monthly meetings again.

Monthly store manager meetings were no longer seen as an unnecessary cost to business but as an investment in building strategy, communicating important information and maintaining a connected environment.

Having well-planned and well-executed monthly store manager meetings at the start of each month is an important strategy for delivering improved results. I do understand that making this happen can be challenging, due to time spent in planning for the meetings and store managers needing to take time away from their stores, but I do believe that store manager meetings must happen every month, without exception.

This suggestion will not be popular with some retailers. There will be resistance based on the store managers' time away from their stores and the cost to the business in extra wages for staff to cover their absence, but I am convinced that this practice can have the greatest positive impact on results.

I often hear that store managers within a region might only get together once or twice a year, mainly due to the cost to the business of doing so more frequently. This flies in the face of research indicating that we work better when we feel part of a community or 'a tribe'. As humans we have a need to feel connected and part of something bigger than our day-to-day work. Monthly store manager meetings help achieve this.

At monthly meetings some of the best ideas are shared, relationships are built and problems are solved. When store managers feel connected, they will call on each other to ask for and offer advice which will mean that not every question will need to be answered and not every problem will need to be solved by you as their area leader.

At monthly meetings, store managers can reflect on the month that was, celebrate successes, address disappointments and move on, to set goals for the new month. Once they have worked together to set their goals as a region and have decided how each individual store will contribute to those goals, you can spend time working with them all together to formulate strategies that will assist in delivering each goal that has been agreed upon for the region.

Without a doubt, the three hours each month spent having a store manager meeting were always my most crucial hours of the month. Putting time and effort into them was time well spent. I would always remind myself of my own sales budget goal for the month ahead and that this was how much my store manager meeting was actually worth to my region.

I would make notes throughout the month and, at the end of the month, I would plan the next month's store manager meeting. I would reflect on:

- 'With what do I want my store managers to walk away from this meeting?'

- 'On what do I need to focus to achieve this?'

- 'What preparation do I need to do for the meeting?'

- 'What preparation do my store managers need to do for the meeting?'

Your monthly store manager meetings also provide you with your best opportunity to implement new systems and strategies, and to communicate important product and marketing initiatives. Various head office/support staff can attend the meetings and present any necessary information to all the store managers from the region at once, which is a far more efficient use of their time. Store managers who might have the same questions will have them all answered at once and all the information will be better communicated to them, which will improve implementation.

Assistant store manager meetings

If you are looking for ways to improve your succession planning and development of future leaders (see Chapter 12), assistant store manager meetings can play an important role in helping you to recognise future leaders. Appointment of sales staff to future leadership roles might be based on informal assessments made at these meetings.

The meetings provide an opportunity to communicate strategies consistent with those of the whole business and consistent with what you are communicating to your store managers. Having these meetings with assistant store managers highlights to them that you value them and that you are invested in their development. You will be amazed at the level of discretionary effort you get from your assistant store managers when they feel valued.

Assistant store manager meetings can be used as training and leadership development sessions. They are a great way to identify when assistant managers are ready to step up and lead their own stores. Investing time and money into assistant managers will pay dividends at a later date, when you are looking to fill store manager roles (more on this in Chapter 12).

Focus groups

Courage is what it takes to stand up and speak; courage is also what it takes to sit down and listen.

Winston Churchill

Focus groups are a fabulous way to gain feedback. Inviting a group of individuals from across your region to provide you with feedback on a particular topic will not only enable you to accumulate valuable insights and information but also improve engagement across the region.

I would regularly facilitate quarterly focus groups of approximately a dozen people from my region. I would decide on a particular topic and invite people I felt were in a position to provide feedback on that topic. Occasionally, I might have a general focus group and ask the questions, 'As an organisation, what do we do well?', and 'What can we do better?'

For a focus group topic, you might select a particular strategy that you are aware needs work in your region or across the organisation. You might want to explore a product strategy for launching a new product. Or, if you are experiencing high staff turnover among your casual staff, you might want to invite a group of casuals to better understand why this could be happening and what could be done to improve their experience.

When staff are invited to focus groups, it makes them feel valued and heard. It elevates their level of engagement because it is interpreted by them as you showing you care about them and what they have to say.

Light bulbs

Actions

Chapter 11

Develop your business acumen

When we think about business acumen, we tend to think about the numbers or the KPIs. These might include sales figures, conversion rates, margins, customer satisfaction or net promoter scores (NPS), costs, and results from staff engagement surveys, etc. These all provide an important window into understanding your region and its results and are crucial if you want to know where to focus when planning and implementing strategies.

I like to think that these numbers, as well as reflecting financial results, are a measure of how well you are looking after your people and your customers.

I have already written earlier about the importance of knowing your numbers and results in order to have effective store visits, so I don't intend focusing on the financial side of business here. There is no doubt that time invested on strategies that are within your control and that impact on your results is time well spent and will serve you and your organisation well.

From a retailer's perspective, there are other areas that I believe should demand your focus if you want to favourably impact your results.

Invest in *all* of your people

People aren't where you save money, they are where you should invest money. Recently, I attended a two-day national retailers' conference. It was a very well-organised event and was well-attended but, when it came to retail strategy, a great amount of the focus was directed towards technology, customer data and logistic systems. Over the two days of the conference, only a one-hour session was focused on people and leadership, which I found extremely disappointing. Having state-of-the-art technology, tracking your customer data and having efficient logistic systems are all important, but nothing happens with any of that without great leadership. From my perspective, that is what matters more than anything if you want to improve your results.

Invest in your locations

I understand the pressure that retailers are under when faced with increasing rents. I also understand that shopping centres need to achieve their revenue budgets and often have unrealistic expectations concerning annual rent increases and the ability of their tenants to pay. This all puts enormous pressures on retail costs.

As a result, many retailers look at ways of reducing their rental costs. One solution is to relocate to a cheaper location. This is evident when you consider the turnover of retailers and the number of vacant stores in major shopping centres, and the relocation of stores to cheaper, less prominent sites within the centre or on a community strip location.

High rents are usually high for a reason. Premises for which the highest rents are charged are usually located in busy shopping centres and are exposed to the most foot traffic, or have the largest shopfront and the best layout. Investing in a prime business location is the best marketing investment in that business that can be made.

That is not to say that rental increases should always be accepted, but there are ways to work around this.

The responsibility for leasing may not be part of many area leaders' roles, but it is still important that you spend some of your time gaining an understanding of leasing, leasing arrangements and the fact that not all leases are created equal. Paying for a good location can be the best marketing investment that can be made for a business.

Case Study: **Location is important**

I was a regular customer at a small women's fashion boutique. It was located on a very busy shopping strip across from a train station, surrounded by buzzing cafés, homeware stores and a very popular day spa. I would wander past on my way to the day spa for my monthly facial and, invariably, would notice something I liked in the window, which would tempt me into the store. Bingo! The retailer would have made a sale!

When I popped in on one occasion, I was surprised to be informed that the retailer was relocating the store because the landlord was increasing her rent and, at her new location, she could save 50% of what she was currently paying.

I spoke to her about the decision and the dangers that it might prove to have for her business. I suggested that she should try to renegotiate further with her landlord or, at least, attempt to find another location in the shopping strip in which the store was already situated.

She was confident that she had a loyal clientele and that they would follow her. She believed the money she would save on rent would help her improve her bottom line.

The new location was on a busy road. However, it only had one other retail store, located next to her – and that was a dog grooming business.

Within twelve months I received a text from her inviting me to her 'closing down sale'.

I was very disappointed for this retailer because she had a great range of women's fashion and did have a loyal clientele.

There had been a couple of times when I had made a special trip to the store if I had needed something for a particular occasion, but most of my purchases had resulted from me just happening to walk by and noticing something in the window. My purchases had largely been impulse purchases.

Value your shopfront

If higher rents are being paid for prominent store locations, it is important to understand that, ultimately, it is the exposure of the shopfront that is being paid for. It is the store's shopfront that will often entice a customer to walk into the store, so the shopfront needs to be valued and utilised to best advantage to ensure the business is getting value for the rent being paid. This means a very strategic approach to what is displayed, ensuring that you display and promote merchandise which your customers are likely to buy.

Case Study: Appeal to what customers want to buy

Recently, I was visiting a coastal Victorian town and noticed in the main street that the local travel agent had a large display in the window promoting tours to South America.

Now this is not to say that South America is not a place people aspire to visit. I admit some people want to travel there, but I am not too sure how many enquiries this promotion would have attracted from passers-by, because there are many other, more popular, destinations to which Australians are more likely to travel.

I was back three months later to see the same display in the same shopfront.

It is important to use your shopfront to attract customers, by advertising what they want to buy rather than what you want to sell.

It is also important to have a welcoming shopfront. The aim is to attract customers into the store. Stores in shopping strip locations should **ALWAYS** have their doors open - even in winter! This advice may not be popular, but research has shown that a customer is more likely to walk into a store if the door is open.

Experiment for yourself. Walk along your own local shopping strip and, when you notice something in a shopfront that catches your eye, pay attention to whether you are more likely to walk into that store if the door is open or shut.

A closed door is a barrier to your business!

Allow your store managers autonomy to make customer-focused decisions

> ### Case Study: **Autonomous decisions**
>
> It was the start of a new season and I was in desperate need of new shoes. I went to my favourite shoe store at my local shopping centre. It's not the cheapest shoe store but always has a fabulous range of shoes, regardless of the season. The store manager was very enthusiastic to help me and showed me a range of shoes that suited my needs.
>
> I tried on four pairs and loved them all. My budget really only stretched as far as two pairs. I cheekily suggested that, if she could give me a small discount, I might try and stretch the budget to three pairs, or even all four. She very politely said that she couldn't because she would 'Get into trouble'. Wow, get into trouble for selling more shoes!
>
> It was 10:00am on a Tuesday morning. I would have thought that a big sale would have been a nice way to start the day.
>
> I said to the shoe store manager 'Can I ask, if this was your business, would you give me a discount?' She immediately replied 'Absolutely!'
>
> I didn't hold this against her. Clearly, she had not been given the autonomy to make a decision that would not only have benefitted me (the customer) but would have contributed a healthy amount towards her sales target for the day. There would also have been the added benefit of increasing her sense of achievement and ownership over the business she was leading as store manager.
>
> As I wandered past a competing shoe store only a few doors down, I noticed that shopfront was advertising: 'Buy one pair and get the second pair half price.'

Aside from me genuinely wanting the shoes, my actions and questions were also a result of the fact that I like to push the sales and service boundaries whenever I can because it often provides me with some further insights into the retail industry as well as a great story to share with my retail clients.

We need to trust our salespeople and allow them to make their own good business decisions. Occasionally they might make a mistake, but the benefit of allowing them to have control of their results will make a great difference to how they feel about the business and how they want to be seen to be performing in their roles.

Understaffing is more costly than overstaffing

Retailers have many systems in place for managing staff costs. From my own work with area leaders, I have found that it is on this that they spend a lot of their time and it is from this that most of their frustration arises. The old saying is true: 'You need to spend money to make money.'

Like many retail customers, I do most of my shopping on a Saturday or Sunday, hoping to get in and out of stores as quickly as possible. I will usually head to one of the major department stores.

I find what I am looking for, then wander around the floor looking for a sales assistant to take my money. As I wander, I might finally find a checkout that is open. I join the long queue and wait … and wait! If I really need what I am buying, I deal with my frustration levels and continue to wait. But, on occasions, I have left the item I wanted to purchase and have walked out.

I recently listened to an address by the chair of the board of a major department store. He explained that the store's results had been disappointing for the first half of the year and, as a result, there would be store closures, investment in online shopping and a focus on products that drove a higher margin.

I couldn't help but think, why not invest in your people and have more staff working when your customers want to buy? Saturdays and Sundays are when foot traffic is at its highest and when customers want to shop. The formula that retailers work from to keep their staff costs down can be flawed and doesn't always make sense. Yes, it does cost more to have more staff on a weekend, but that is when your customers want to buy and when there is the greatest opportunity to increase your sales.

I often read about retailers wanting to improve the customer experience. This staffing strategy alone could change the performance of a retailer.

Sales results, KPIs and budget achievements are less about the numbers themselves and more about the choices we make. They are also about area leaders being able to see the impact that the choices they make or don't make can have on results.

Different organisations allow different levels of autonomy to their area leaders. Having worked with many area leaders from a variety of retailers and businesses, I have come to realise that they largely believe they do not have the authority to make decisions. Yet, when they ask for what they need, they are often surprised when the response they are given is 'Yes' and their request is met!

Regardless of the autonomy you feel you have or don't have, think about the decisions you can and should make. If you are unsure, it is best to speak to your leader about ideas or strategies on which you would like to act or that you would like to put in place.

It is better to put forward an idea and have it rejected than not to put any ideas forward at all.

Light bulbs

Actions

Chapter 12

STRATEGY 7

Develop your future leaders

If there is one thing I have learnt from my years as an area leader and the time I have spent working with area leaders since then it is that what causes area leaders most distress and increases their workload is not having all of their stores led by effective store managers.

When a store is operating without an onsite leader this can result in: a lack of focus on customers; brand standards not being upheld; no one being held accountable for working towards achieving sales budgets; and difficulty managing rosters. Ultimately the area leader will be required to spend more time in that store, managing the day-to-day activities usually carried out by the store manager. This results in the area leader having less time for her/his other stores.

The root cause of a lack of effective store managers is a lack of succession planning and development of future leaders.

Usually the ascension of store managers and area leaders looks like this:

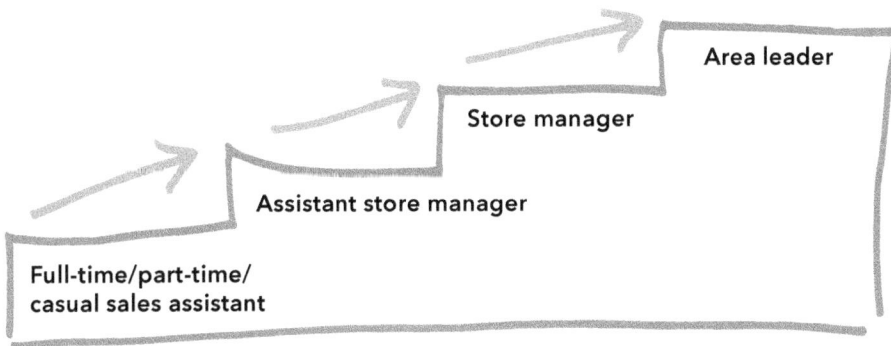

Area leader

Store manager

Assistant store manager

Full-time/part-time/
casual sales assistant

The key to a happy life as an area leader is for all stores in your region to have store managers who are motivated and engaged. The only way to manage this is to have a consistent focus on succession planning and the development of future leaders. As an area leader this was one of my most important strategies and I emphasise this now when I am coaching or working with a group of area leaders. Completing a health check of where potential leaders currently are in their development and putting a plan in place to continue to develop them is a must.

Without focusing on succession planning and developing future leaders, when a vacancy arises you could be forced to fill store manager roles with unsuitable or inexperienced people. Some of those people might have never even wanted to be leaders, so will lack the drive and motivation for the roles. Appointing these people to store manager roles might solve immediate staffing problems but it does create the potential for other problems to arise in the future.

Without a focus on succession planning and developing future leaders, you might also be forced to recruit externally for store managers, which is not only costly but also time-consuming. Your valuable time will be taken up by recruiting and interviewing, as well as inducting the new recruits and training them on business systems, product knowledge and brand standards. Ideally, to avoid this, you want store managers to be appointed from within the organisation. This also sends a positive message to the staff in your region that they can have a career in leadership if they desire.

If you focus long-term on a succession plan and the development of future leaders this can all be avoided.

Some strategies that might help you are outlined in the remainder of this chapter.

The role of the assistant store manager

Assistant store managers play an important role in supporting the store manager, but they play an even more important role for the area leader. A key to ensuring you have new store managers ready to step up is to ensure you have a team of competent assistant store managers in place.

Too often, assistant store managers are appointed without really understanding their roles. Yes, they are meant to support store managers but, just as importantly, their role represents an apprenticeship for them to become future store managers themselves.

If you have a team of assistant store managers who do not have the desire to be store managers, this will cause you problems when you need to fill store manager roles. So, when you are recruiting assistant store managers, you must ensure that a large proportion of the people you appoint want to lead their own stores. This matter needs to be addressed and understood during the recruitment process. It is a crucial strategy that, when carried out well, makes succession planning easy.

Identifying bright, keen and enthusiastic staff in the early days of them joining your region means you are able to create a leadership pathway for them. They can see, from their early days, they have a future in your business. The most successful store managers have usually developed some of their skills by spending time as assistant store managers.

Developing your assistant store managers

The time and money you invest in developing your assistant store managers will pay dividends down the track. You might invest in quarterly training sessions; or in them attending focus groups; or in providing specific projects for which they are responsible, such as a local store marketing initiative, training a new staff member or driving promotion of a particular product, etc.

The best time for developing and inspiring this important group of future leaders is during your store visits – spending time with them, getting to know them, career planning with them one-on-one and giving them a sense that their role is important. When you start to give their important role more focus in this way, more people will begin to see it as an attractive and valued role in the business and will aspire to take it on.

Assistant store manager focus groups

I have already highlighted the importance of assistant store manager meetings (in Chapter 10). Asking assistant store managers to participate in focus groups can also be a great way to gain feedback on future business strategies.

I held quarterly focus groups and at least one of them would be specifically for assistant store managers to gain insights into how the business could be improved. I found that groups of assistant store managers often had valuable information and feedback to share, and the focus groups provided a vehicle for me to hear and implement some of their ideas.

Having multiple assistant store managers

Most retailers will have some stores that are particularly busy, trading seven days a week. These are sometimes known as 'flagship' stores. These stores require more staff, juggling multiple shifts, and provide an opportunity to have multiple assistant store managers who can lead the way in the stores and learn the ropes at the same time - fulfilling their apprenticeship. Some retailers are reluctant to adopt this approach because they see it as a cost, but I feel it is far more costly to fail to have a solid succession and development plan. The more grounding that can be given to assistant store managers as leaders, the better it is for the business long-term.

Light bulbs

Actions

Chapter 13

Conclusion

I will never forget the excitement I felt when I received the call from Geoff Harris to let me know that I had 'got the job' when he appointed me to the role of Flight Centre Travel Group's first area leader in Victoria. My elation at starting a new role was mixed with the sadness of leaving my store team who had become like my second family. But I also couldn't wait for the opportunity to show other store managers how to achieve the results I had been able to achieve. I felt like I could change the world! I knew how to run a successful store so, surely, it would be just a matter of telling those other store managers what to do so they could achieve the same results as me - or so I thought!

Over the following few years my excitement and enthusiasm turned to frustration and I was overwhelmed. I wish someone had written this book back then, so I could have referred to it. It would have been like having a mentor who related to my struggles and could guide me, prepare me, teach me the new skills I needed to learn and the shift in mindset I would need to make, and help me understand how different the area leader role would be to that of the store manager role I had left.

I can't help but think of all of the potentially successful area leaders who have stepped away from their roles as a result of not receiving the right training and guidance to adapt their approach to leadership - to start leading through influence, rather than through control.

From a business perspective, millions of dollars have been invested over the years in recruiting area leaders to their roles, but not much has been invested to develop them in the roles and set them up for success.

In my own coaching and training business and, now, in this book, I have attempted to share my own experience of being an area leader and of leading area leaders. I have found there are four general categories into which area leaders can be seen to fit, according to how they deliver on support and expectations (see Chapter 2).

1   'Accommodating' area leaders (providing high support and having low expectations)

2   'Controlling' area leaders (providing low support and having high expectations)

3   'Stagnating' area leaders (providing low support and having low expectations)

4   'Empowering' area leaders (providing high support and having high expectations)

Area leaders categorised as 'empowering' usually find a balance between the creation of a great working environment and implementation of strategies that achieve results. Becoming a leader of this type is the goal at which to aim. But 'empowering' area leaders don't suddenly appear. Typically, they evolve through some experience of behaviours from the other three categories of area leadership, often starting as accommodating (high support, low expectations) and evolving through experience.

If you seek out the necessary support and specific training to become an 'empowering' area leader, you will come to see the resolution of many of the issues you face in your role.

If you are not achieving what you want to achieve in the role, I hope you have found some answers in the pages of this book. But, from my own experience, the best place to start is focusing on improving the environment within your region. Building a great business starts with the business environment but, often, this aspect is the most neglected.

The role of every business leader should be to create an environment of which everyone wants to be a part; an environment in which people feel valued, appreciated and part of a community. To achieve this, there is a need for leaders to learn the softer skills of leadership, such as empathy and an understanding of the importance of relationships and connection.

All of the following are important in building a healthy business environment:

1   a common vision

2   building/valuing relationships

3   harnessing connection

4   creating ownership

5   valuing and appreciating people (all of them).

When you have the right environment, implementing strategies becomes easier because your teams are happy, engaged and want the organisation to do well.

Key strategies I have found to work for an area leader are:

- **Strategy 1:** Prioritise and manage your time (see Chapter 6)
  Allow time for the unexpected and don't overschedule your time; avoid spending an unwarranted amount of time in stores; spend time planning, preparing and establishing key outcomes for store visits; and prioritise your activities.

- **Strategy 2:** Maximise your store visits (see Chapter 7)
  The best results occur when store managers are allowed to develop into true business leaders, taking spiritual and psychological ownership of their stores. Allow and encourage them to do this when you visit their stores.

- **Strategy 3:** Deliver on your store visits (see Chapter 8)
  It is the quality not the quantity of store visits that matters. Be prepared and organised; carefully schedule and prioritise the stores you need to visit; prepare a business folder for each store; be clear of purpose; and follow up on the implementation of strategies discussed at the visits.

- **Strategy 4:** Engage your part-time workforce (see Chapter 9)
  Aim at making all staff, including the casual and part-time employees, feel valued, appreciated and cared about.

- **Strategy 5:** Have meetings that matter (see Chapter 10)
  Get the right information to the right people at the right time. Area leaders are responsible for ensuring all of the important information from various parts of the business reach the store managers so that they are all informed.

- **Strategy 6:** Develop your business acumen (see Chapter 11)
  Invest in all of your people; invest in locations, value your shopfront, and realise that understaffing is costly. Realise the impact that the choices you make or don't make can have on results.

- **Strategy 7:** Develop your future leaders (see Chapter 12)
  Succession planning and development of future leaders is important for the future of your organisation.

Results are what we are all in business to achieve. However, as much as we want to achieve those results, they are really the outcome of how well we manage to provide a happy and productive workplace environment and how well we can implement our strategies.

Whether your organisation has a focus on developing area leaders or not, you can take responsibility for your own development. I have always focused on my own personal and professional development, rather than waiting for the organisation employing me to take on that responsibility.

Regardless of your budget there is a lot you can do to develop yourself as a business leader, such as: read books (like this one), listen to podcasts, find mentors within your own organisation, engage a leadership coach or seek suitable training from an expert in the specific skills you want to development.

This book was designed as a practical guide, containing lots of strategies to help you. It might be helpful to go back and reread the whole book or to reread certain sections containing the information on which you want to focus. If you have taken the opportunity to fill in your 'Light bulbs' and 'Actions' at the end of the chapters throughout this book, you already have some specific areas to reflect on and strategies to implement.

I sincerely hope that I have been able to convey to you the important role you play in your organisation and that you are worth investing in. Now, more than ever, retail needs great leadership!

Afterword: Work with me

My hope is that reading this book might be the catalyst you needed to make a change in the way you lead. If change for the better is what you seek, then implementing some of what you have read here will assist.

I am committed to working with retail managers and leaders to deliver genuine growth in the people they employ and to deliver results for their businesses.

If you would like to develop your skills as an area leader further, I extend an invitation for you to work with me. You can do this in a range of ways. All of the information in this book can be unpacked and developed further through a range of webinars, workshops, programs and one-on-one coaching sessions provided by Alison Crabb Consulting.

If you are part of a larger retailer network and would like to discuss a bespoke program for your retail leadership team, please get in touch.

Visit my website: www.alisoncrabb.com.au

Contact me: alison@alisoncrabb.com.au

MENTOR AND COACHING PROGRAMS

A feature of great leaders is that they never stop learning. Mentorship and coaching for leaders is a sound business investment which can positively impact on your entire organisation and the people you lead.

While the specific challenges faced by individual leaders vary, the one-on-one coaching process invariably allows leaders to improve their capabilities and results, to experience greater satisfaction and to become at ease in their roles due to them becoming more skilled and ready to respond to opportunities as they arise.

You can benefit from complete access to my experience and support from the training programs I offer, or from bespoke coaching programs I design to focus on your individual needs over a timeframe that is right for your goals.

WORKSHOPS

If a key element of your organisation appears to be limiting the engagement or performance of the people you employ, my workshops are designed to get your organisation moving quickly towards better results.

I personally facilitate every session, ensuring that the learning is tailored to your needs and you have not only the benefit of my expertise but also my direct support.

Over time, I have observed the incredible impact of targeted training on the areas which hold businesses back. Half-day and full-day workshops can be tailored to target issues faced by your business, to ensure that the best outcomes for you are achieved.

LEADERSHIP PROGRAMS

My range of leadership programs have been designed to take retail leadership to a new level. As much as we all want to achieve results, those results are really the outcome of how well we manage to provide a happy and productive workplace environment and how well we can implement our business strategies.

My leadership programs expand and elaborate on the contents of this book, providing deeper understanding and learning, in a timeframe that allows you to work on one strategy at a time.

KEYNOTE SPEAKING AND CONFERENCE WORKSHOPS

Do you have an upcoming conference you would like to use as a vehicle to provide training for your team?

My delivery of keynote presentations and group training at conferences has proven to be an effective way for me to share inspirational, actionable insights with diverse audiences.

As a tailored offering, the presentations I deliver can be adapted to reflect your organisation's conference theme and key focuses.

EVENTS AND WEBINARS

Please see my website for upcoming events, webinars and workshops on a range of topics relating to leadership and retail operations.

For more details visit: www.alisoncrabb.com.au

Glossary

'accommodating' area leaders
a category of area leaders who provide their store managers and staff with high levels of support but have low expectations for the store/area results, being more concerned with relationships than results

area leader
a business employee whose role it is to oversee several retail outlets within an organisation (sometimes called a multi-site manager; a regional leader; a regional manager or a cluster manager)

assistant store manager
the store employees employed in supporting positions to store managers; they have the potential to be store managers in the future

brand
a name, term, design, symbol, or any other feature that identifies one retailer's goods or services as distinct from those of other retailers

business strategy
see strategy

cluster manager
see area leader

'controlling' area leaders
a category of area leaders who provide their store managers and staff with low levels of support but have high expectations for store/area results, tending to take over control at store level to achieve desired results

conversion rates
measures of the proportion of visitors to a retail outlet who make a purchase

customer data
information held on file about customers by a store or other business, usually including names, contact details, and buying habits

customer satisfaction
a measurement that determines how happy customers are with a retailer's products, services, and capabilities

discretionary effort
the level of effort people are willing to give above and beyond the minimum required

'empowering' area leaders	a category of area leaders who provide their store managers and staff with high levels of support and have high expectations for the store/area results, striking a happy balance between a harmonious work environment and strategies to achieve results
environment	As well as referring to the surrounding circumstances, objects, or conditions in the usual way, the term is used in this book to refer to the intangible, unquantifiable quality of a workplace and work situation that makes it a good place to work
expectations (for the area leader role)	that which is expected of stores and personnel by area leaders; and is expected of area leaders by store managers
fixed mindset	the belief that we each have a certain skillset and are only capable of what comes naturally, with no opportunity to change or to improve
growth mindset	the belief that we can keep growing and developing if we are open to change and look for possibilities; that we have the capacity to improve and grow
inventory	property, goods in stock, or the contents of a store
key performance indicators (KPIs)	quantifiable measures used to evaluate the success of an organisation or employee in meeting objectives
levelling up	to progress or advance to the next level
logistic systems	a network of organisations, people, activities, information and resources involved in the physical flow of products from supplier to customer
margin	the differences between the price a retailer pays for an item and the price at which the item is sold to customers
merchandising	the activity of promoting the sale of goods, especially by their presentation in retail outlets
multi-site manager	*see* area leader

net promoter score (NPS)	an index ranging from –100 to 100 that measures the willingness of customers to recommend a company's products or services to others
one-on-ones	face-to-face meetings between two people
regional leader	*see* area leader
regional manager	*see* area leader
sales figures	the value or amount of the total sales of products for a particular period
staff engagement surveys	surveys designed to measure and assess how motivated and engaged employees are to perform their best at work each day
'stagnating' area leaders	a category of area leaders who provide their store managers and staff with low levels of support and have low expectations for store/area results
state leader	The employee who oversees and leads the area leaders and whose region includes all the smaller regions in a state. These leaders are responsible for a range of activities, including staff education, professional development, policy, advocacy, communication, marketing, sponsorship, finance and administration.
store manager	the employee in a managerial role in a store, who is responsible for staff and their wellbeing; presentation of advertising and store displays; recruitment, performance management and workplace scheduling; and product management, including ordering, receiving, and price changes
strategy	a summary of how the organisation will achieve its goals, meet the expectations of its customers and sustain a competitive advantage in the marketplace
support (provided by area leaders)	delivery to store managers of the tools and training they require to do their jobs and deliver on expectations
working on business (WOB) days	contrasting with working *in* business days, these are days spent planning and reflecting (rather than working in the field)

About the author

Alison Crabb, founder and principal of Alison Crabb Consulting, has worked with some of Australia's most recognised and successful retailers for more than 30 years. Her career in the retail industry began as a travel consultant with the Flight Centre Travel Group, where her promotion first to store manager and then to an area leadership role was to eventually see her spend eight years as a global leader in a highly competitive and challenging retail environment.

Through these years of learning, development and improvement, Alison continued to push the boundaries and drive improvement year on year, seeing profit grow from $18 million to $49 million. The culture of excellence Alison was instrumental in building at Flight Centre during her years of leadership led to her division being the most profitable division globally for eight consecutive years. She achieved unprecedented results working with more than 1200 staff across more than 200 retail outlets, generating $1.2 billion in sales annually.

Alison's achievements were recognised when she was awarded Flight Centre's Directors' Award for Global Outstanding Achievement in 2010. She was also a finalist in the Telstra Businesswoman of the Year Award in 2012.

Since leaving Flight Centre to begin her own retail consulting business, Alison has worked in a coaching and consultancy role with some of Australia's leading retail businesses, developing and lifting their leadership to achieve new business heights. Throughout her career, Alison's business reputation has been built on knowledge, experience, trust and success.

Alison Crabb is recognised by many to be the industry's leading expert on retail leadership. In her consultancy role with Alison Crabb Consulting, Alison has designed a unique, refreshing, personalised and highly engaging, retail-centric approach to leadership training and development. Her 30 years of experience in consumer led retail has provided her with invaluable insights into the factors influencing retail success and the keys to achieving and delivering them.

For more details, visit: www.alisoncrabb.com.au

or email Alison: alison@alisoncrabb.com.au